Contents

Introduction

About the course

During this course you must study four units:
- **Unit 1** International Relations: The era of the Cold War 1943–1991
- **Unit 2** Modern World Depth Study
- **Unit 3** Modern World Source Enquiry
- **Unit 4** Representations of History

These are assessed through three examination papers and one controlled assessment:
- In Unit 1 you have one hour and 15 minutes to answer questions on International Relations: The era of the Cold War 1943–1991.
- In Unit 2 you have one hour and 15 minutes to answer questions on a Modern World Depth Study.
- In Unit 3 you have one hour and 15 minutes to answer questions based on sources on one Modern World Source Enquiry topic.
- In the controlled assessment you have to complete a task under controlled conditions in the classroom (Unit 4).

About the book

This book has been written to support option 3a 'War and the transformation of British society 1903–1928' in Unit 3. It covers the key developments in Britain from 1903 to 1928. The book is divided into four key topics, each with three chapters:
- **Key Topic 1** examines British society in the years before the First World War, including the campaign by different women's societies for the vote and the reactions of the Liberal government. In addition it explains the important social reforms introduced during these years.
- **Key Topic 2** explains the part played by the British on the Western Front, including the role of the BEF in 1914, the trench system, new weapons and methods and the importance of

Haig and the Somme, as well as Britain's contribution to the defeat of Germany in 1918.
- **Key Topic 3** examines the specific impact of the war on the Home Front, including the change in the role of government, as well as recruitment, conscription and rationing and the changing role of women.
- **Key Topic 4** looks at Britain in the ten years after the First World War, especially further changes in the role of women and the industrial unrest which culminated in the General Strike of 1926.

Each chapter in this book:
- Contains activities – some develop the historical skills you will need, others are exam-style questions that give you the opportunity to practise exam skills.
- Gives step-by-step guidance, model answers and advice on how to answer particular question types in Unit 3.
- Highlights glossary terms in bold the first time they appear in each key topic.

About Unit 3

Unit 3 is a test of:
- The ability to answer a range of source-based questions.
- Knowledge and understanding of the key developments in each of the four key topics.

The examination paper will contain six or seven sources, including:
- Written sources, such as extracts from diaries, speeches, letters, poems, songs, biographies, autobiographies, memoirs, newspapers, modern history textbooks, and the views of historians.
- Illustrations, such as photographs, posters, cartoons and paintings.

Below is a set of specimen questions (without the sources). You will be given step-by-step guidance throughout the book on how best to approach and answer these types of questions.

This is an **inference** question. You have to get a message or messages from the source.

This question asks you to explain the **purpose** of a representation. What is its message? Why was it produced?

This is an **explanation** question. You have to use the source and what you have learned and remembered to give an explanation.

This is a **reliability** question. It is asking you to decide how reliable each source is, and to compare their reliability.

This is an **interpretation** question. It is asking you to use some or all of the sources, and what you know about the topic, to judge how far you agree with an interpretation which you have been given.

UNIT 3 EXAM

1   Study Source A.
    What can you learn from Source A about the early stages of the Battle of the Somme?
    (6 marks)

2   Study Source C and use your own knowledge.
    What is the purpose of this representation? Use details from the representation and your own knowledge to explain your answer.
    (8 marks)

3   Study Source A and use your own knowledge.
    Use Source A and your own knowledge to explain why the German Schlieffen Plan failed.
    (10 marks)

4   Study Sources D and E.
    How reliable are Sources D and E as evidence of a gas attack on the Western Front? Explain your answer using Sources D and E and your own knowledge.
    (10 marks)

5   Study Sources A, E and F and use your own knowledge.

    Spelling, punctuation and grammar will be assessed in this question.

    Source A suggests that Red Friday was the main reason for the outbreak of the General Strike of 1926.

    How far do you agree with this interpretation? Use your own knowledge, Sources A, E and F and any other sources you find helpful to explain your answer.
    (16 marks)

    (Total for spelling, punctuation and grammar = 3 marks)
    (Total for question 5 = 19 marks)

Key Topic 1: The Liberals, votes for women and social reform

Task

Study Source A. What can you learn from Source A about Lloyd George's attitude to helping the poor?

This key topic examines the way in which women challenged successive governments in the early twentieth century in their attempt to gain the vote. The campaigns of the **suffragists** and **suffragettes** are analysed and the position of women by 1914 is examined in detail.

The topic also looks at the impact of the publication of the Booth and Rowntree reports, which investigated the extent of poverty in Britain, and how the **Liberals** then accepted that the government should play a more active role in the welfare of its citizens.

Each chapter explains a key issue and examines important lines of enquiry as outlined below:

Chapter 1 The activities of the women's societies and the reaction of the authorities (pages 5–16)

- What was the political position of women in 1903?
- What methods were used by the women's societies to campaign for the vote?
- How did the authorities react to the activities of the women's societies?
- Why had women not been given the vote by 1914?

Chapter 2 Children's welfare measures and old age pensions (pages 17–24)

- Why were reforms introduced to help children and the old?

- What were the key features of the reforms for children?
- What were the key features of the Old Age Pensions Act?

Chapter 3 Labour Exchanges and the National Insurance Act (pages 25–29)

- What were Labour Exchanges and why were they set up?
- Why was the National Insurance Act introduced?
- What were the key features of the National Insurance scheme?

The activities of the women's societies and the reaction of the authorities

Source A: A leaflet published by the National Union of Women's Suffrage Societies (NUWSS) in the early 1900s

Task

Study Source A and use your own knowledge. Why was this leaflet so widely distributed? Use details from the leaflet and your own knowledge to explain the answer.

In 1903 women in Britain had few political rights. They could not vote or stand for Parliament. In the years that followed, three societies campaigned for the vote, using methods that varied from peaceful and law-abiding by the suffragists to more extreme and militant methods by the suffragettes. The Liberal government reacted by arresting some suffragettes and force-feeding those who carried out hunger strikes.

This chapter answers the following questions:

• What was the political position of women in 1903?
• What methods were used by the women's societies to campaign for the vote?
• How did the authorities react to the activities of the women's societies?
• Why had women not been given the vote by 1914?

Examination skills

In this chapter you will be given guidance on how to answer the inference question, Question 1, which is worth six marks.

What was the political position of women in 1903?

In 1901, Queen Victoria died. She had been a strong opponent of women's rights and, at the beginning of the twentieth century, women in Britain played little part in political life. They were not able to vote in general elections or stand for Parliament. However, at this time there were powerful arguments emerging for and against votes for women, as shown in the box below. Several politicians such as Keir Hardie, leader of the Labour Party, and Lloyd George, a Liberal, supported votes for women, whereas others – including several leading Conservatives – were opposed to it.

Source A: From a speech by Queen Victoria

'This mad, wicked folly of women's rights. With the vote, women would become the most hateful, heartless and disgusting of human beings. Where would be the protection which man was intended to give to the weaker sex?

Source B: From *Working women and the Suffrage*, written by Mrs Wibaut in 1900

The working woman needs the vote in order to obtain better houses, better conditions of living, shorter hours of work, better care for her children.

Tasks

1. *Study Source A. What can you learn from Source A about the attitude of Queen Victoria towards votes for women?*

2. *What reasons are suggested in Source B for votes for women?*

3. *Draw two mind maps:*

- *one showing the reasons for opposition to votes for women*
- *the other showing the reasons for support for votes for women.*

On each mind map, place the reasons in rank order of importance, beginning with the most important at 12 o'clock, with the others clockwise in rank order. Explain your choices.

Arguments opposing votes for women	Arguments supporting votes for women
• Men and women have different interests and responsibilities. Women are home-makers and mothers, whereas a man's role is to debate and make decisions. • Women do not fight in wars for their country so why should they have a say in whether the country should go to war? • Women are pure, so they need to be protected from the corrupt world of politics. • Giving middle-class women the vote will encourage them to develop careers and neglect their family duties. • Women are too emotional to be trusted with the responsibility of the vote.	• Women have been allowed to vote in local elections since 1888. If they are good enough to vote in local elections, then why not general elections? • Other parts of the British Empire, including New Zealand, have already given the vote to women so Britain should do the same. • Women pay taxes, just like men, and therefore should be allowed to influence MPs, through voting, on how the money should be spent. • Many single women and widows have the same financial responsibilities as men, so they should have the same political rights. • Women have special skills, expertise and interests which could help and influence Parliament to make better laws on issues such as education and the family.

The Liberals, votes for women and social reform

What methods were used by the women's societies to campaign for the vote?

The campaign for votes for women really intensified in the years after the death of Queen Victoria due to the activities of three different women's societies: the **NUWSS**, the **WSPU** and the **WFL**.

The NUWSS

The National Union of Women's Suffrage Societies (NUWSS) was set up in 1897 by Millicent Fawcett and had nearly 500 branches throughout the country.

Fawcett was a suffragist. Suffragists believed that women would get the vote eventually. Indeed, she described the campaign for the vote as being like a glacier – slow but unstoppable. All they had to do was keep on the right side of the law and do all they could to persuade Parliament that their cause was just; peaceful methods would prove that women deserved the vote.

The NUWSS issued pamphlets, presented petitions and organised marches and meetings. Millicent thought it was crucial to keep the issue in the public eye. At every election suffragists questioned the candidates on their attitude to women's **suffrage**. By 1900 they had achieved some success, gaining the support of a number of Liberal MPs as well as a few Conservatives and the newly formed Labour Party.

They continued to use peaceful methods throughout the early twentieth century and organised a series of marches to London, including:
- The 1907 Hyde Park 'mud march'. On 9 February about 4000 women walked from Hyde Park to the Exeter Hall in the Strand. Unfortunately it poured with rain all day and the long skirts and dresses of the women were soon covered with mud.
- In 1913 they organised a **pilgrimage**, with women marching to London from eight different directions. At the final meeting on 26 July 1913, held in Hyde Park, there were nineteen different platforms for speakers.

By 1914, membership of the NUWSS had reached 50,000. They collected £50,000 annually and had their own newspaper called *The Common Cause*. With the outbreak of the First World War, Millicent Fawcett suspended the activities of the suffragists and used the NUWSS to help with the war effort, especially the recruitment of volunteers.

> **Source A: From an article in the *Manchester Guardian*, 10 February 1907**
>
> *Nobody can suppose that most of the women who took part [in the march] … can have done so for sport or for the pleasure of the thing … it requires some courage for a woman to step out of her drawing room into the street to take her place in a mixed throng for a cause probably distasteful to many or most of her acquaintances, and to see herself pilloried in the newspaper the next morning by name as one of the suffragettes.*

> **Source B: Millicent Fawcett making a speech at a mass meeting in Hyde Park in 1913**

Task

1. *How reliable are Sources A and B as evidence of the activities of the NUWSS? Explain your answer using Sources A and B and your own knowledge.*

The WSPU

Some supporters of votes for women became frustrated with the gradual, even slow approach of the suffragists. As a result, in 1903 Mrs Emmeline Pankhurst founded a new organisation, the Women's Social and Political Union (WSPU) which was determined to use more extreme, even militant, methods to get publicity and secure the vote more quickly. The *Daily Mail* nicknamed these more extreme campaigners 'suffragettes', and the name stuck.

Emmeline Pankhurst had been married to Dr Richard Pankhurst, a politician and lawyer. Before he died in 1898, he had encouraged his wife to work for rights for women. She was supported by her daughters Christabel and Sylvia.

Interrupting political meetings 1905–1906

WSPU militancy began in 1905 when they decided to target political meetings by leading Liberals during the general election campaign of that year. The Liberals seemed more likely to win, so it was important to know whether they would give the vote to women.

During a Liberal meeting on 13 October 1905 in Manchester where Sir Edward Grey, the Foreign Secretary, was due to speak, Christabel Pankhurst stood up and asked the question 'Will you give votes to women?' She refused to sit down when he didn't answer, and was dragged out of the hall and arrested for pretending to spit at a policeman. Other meetings were interrupted, followed by further arrests.

Source C: Emmeline Pankhurst describes one of the public demonstrations by the WSPU in 1905, at a meeting addressed by the Prime Minister

At the end of the meeting, Annie Kenney, whom we had smuggled into the hall in disguise, called out in her clear, sweet voice: 'Will the Liberal Government give women the vote?' At the same moment, Theresa Billingham let drop a huge banner with the words: 'Will the Liberal Government do justice to working women?' Just for a moment there was a gasping silence, the people waiting to see what the Cabinet Ministers would do. They did nothing. Then amid uproar and shouting, the women were seized and flung out of the hall.

Prison and hunger striking

On 5 July 1909, the imprisoned suffragette Marion Wallace Dunlop, a sculptor and illustrator, went on hunger strike. She had been sent to Holloway Prison for printing an extract from the Bill of Rights (introduced in 1689 to protect the rights of citizens) on the wall of St Stephen's Hall in the House of Commons. In her second division cell, Wallace Dunlop declined all food as a protest against the authorities' refusal to recognise her as a political prisoner. (Being a political prisoner would have entitled her to be placed in the first division where inmates enjoyed certain privileges.) After three and a half days of fasting, she was released.

Other suffragettes that summer of 1909, believing they had found a powerful weapon with which to fight a stubborn Liberal government, also went on hunger strike. However, the government feared that the early release of such rebellious prisoners would make a mockery of the justice system and by the end of September **force-feeding** was introduced (see page 11).

Source D: A photograph showing Emmeline and Christabel Pankhurst in prison clothes. It was posed for a suffragette display in 1913

The Liberals, votes for women and social reform

Window smashing

In March 1912 the WSPU began a stone-throwing campaign in the centre of London to gain even more publicity for the cause of votes for women. They targeted expensive shops in Oxford Street, Regent Street and around Piccadilly Circus, hoping that the shop owners would pressurise the Liberal government into giving votes to women to prevent further attacks. At 4p.m. on 1 March, suffragettes broke thousands of windows and 219 suffragettes were arrested. A few days later, shops in Kensington were attacked in the same way.

Source E: A notice outside a jeweller's shop in 1912

Ladies, if we had the power to grant it, you should have the vote right away. Please do not smash these windows; they are not insured.

WSPU METHODS

Emily Davison

Emily Wilding Davison, from Morpeth in Northumberland, was an experienced suffragette campaigner. She had been in prison nine times for setting fire to post boxes and even a post office. She targeted the world-famous horse race, the Derby, at Epsom. In order to get maximum publicity on 5 June 1913, she decided to rush out and pin a suffragette banner on the King's horse, Anmer. As the horses rounded Tattenham corner, she rushed in front of Anmer, only to be hit by the horse and killed. Her funeral, ten days later, was attended by thousands of suffragettes who saw it as a major celebration of her ultimate sacrifice.

Source F: From an article in *The Times* newspaper, 6 June 1913

The woman rushed from the rails as the horse swept round Tattenham Corner. She did not interfere with the racing but she nearly killed the jockey as well as herself as she brought down a valuable horse. A deed of this kind is unlikely to increase the popularity of the women's cause.

Other types of militancy

In the years 1912–14 the suffragettes used many violent methods. They cut telephone wires, set fire to derelict buildings and post boxes, poured purple dye into reservoirs, poured acid on the greens of golf courses and slashed paintings in art galleries. They frequently attacked and assaulted leading Liberals, especially Herbert Henry Asquith who had become Prime Minister in 1908.

Source G: Mary Richardson explaining why she tried to use an axe to destroy a famous painting, called *The Rokeby Venus*, in the National Gallery, London

I have tried to destroy the picture of the most beautiful woman in mythological history because the government are destroying Mrs Pankhurst, the most beautiful character in modern history.

Tasks

2. *How reliable are Sources C and F as evidence of the activities of the suffragettes? Explain your answer using Sources C and F and your own knowledge.*

3. *Study Source G. What can you learn from Source G about the methods used by the suffragettes?*

4. *Study Source D and use your own knowledge. What was the purpose of this photograph? Use details from the photograph and your own knowledge to answer the question.*

The WFL

The Women's Freedom League (WFL) was set up in 1907 by leading members of the Women's Social and Political Union (WSPU) who began to question the leadership of Christabel Pankhurst. They objected to the way the Pankhursts were making decisions without consulting members, as well as their more extreme campaigning methods (see pages 8–9). The leader was Charlotte Despard, a well-known novelist who had devoted much time and money to helping the poor in Battersea.

The Women's Freedom League grew rapidly, and soon had sixty branches throughout Britain with an overall membership of about 4000 people. The WFL also established its own newspaper, *The Vote*. Members were not as peaceful as the suffragists and were prepared to break the law as long as it did not lead to violence.

Their methods included:

- Refusing to take part in the census in 1911, the official population count. They broke the law by refusing to fill in the census form. Some women spent the night away from home, or stayed in empty houses, in order to make the census inaccurate. The magazine *Punch* wrote that such ladies 'had taken leave of their census'.
- Chaining themselves to the railings outside the House of Commons. In 1907 some members chained themselves to the grille of the ladies' gallery in the House of Commons and shouted 'votes for women'. The grille had to be removed and these ladies sat in a committee room until a locksmith came and released them.
- **Picketing** MPs. From 3 July to 28 October 1909, WFL ladies with banners and leaflets sat outside the House of Commons whenever it was in session and picketed MPs.
- Organising marches and demonstrations, including a march from Edinburgh to London.
- Refusing to pay taxes, arguing that they were not represented in Parliament. For this, their property was sold to pay what they owed.
- High-profile stunts. For example, Muriel Matters, a member of the WFL, hired an airship and flew over the Houses of Parliament, throwing out carrots and propaganda leaflets.

Source H: From a description by the novelist H G Wells, who observed women outside the House of Commons in 1907

There were grey-headed old ladies standing there, sturdily charming in the rain; north country factory girls; cheaply dressed suburban women; trim, comfortable mothers of families; valiant-eyed university students; lank, hungry-looking creatures who stirred one's imagination.

Source I: A photograph of the WFL's touring publicity caravan, taken in 1910

WOMEN'S FREEDOM LEAGUE.
1, ROBERT STREET, ADELPHI, W.C., and 30, Gordon Street, Glasgow.

VOTES FOR WOMEN.

"A HALT NEAR CHICHESTER."   PHOTO BY WINIFRED TURNER.

Tasks

5. Study Source H. What can you learn from Source H about the members of the WFL?

6. Study Source I and use your own knowledge. Why do you think this photograph was publicised widely? Use details from the photograph and your own knowledge to explain the answer.

7. Devise a catchy newspaper headline for a report about the WFL airship.

8. Which of the methods used by the WFL do you think would have been most effective? Explain your answer.

How did the authorities react to the activities of the women's societies?

The Liberal government had to deal with the problems of hunger-striking and increasing suffragette militancy. They did so through the force-feeding of hunger strikers and a number of government bills.

Force-feeding

The prison authorities were afraid that a suffragette might die in prison, and this would give them even more publicity, so they began force-feeding. To force-feed a hunger striker, prison officers pushed a tube down her throat and into her stomach. They then poured liquid food down the tube. In this way, a suffragette on hunger strike was kept alive. This brought bad publicity for the Liberal government and aroused sympathy for the suffragette prisoners.

Source A: A suffragette, Mary Richardson, describes being force-fed in 1909

> There is a wardress holding each shoulder, two at each arm, two at the sides, and these kneel on your ribs until your breathing shows a dangerous shortness. Sheets are flung over you, one over your head and forehead, another wardress holds your head and presses her thumbs into your temple. The doctor enters and you see his hands at work on the tubes in front of your half-shut eyes. He puts the tube carefully into the nose but then thrusts it with violence into a small nasal opening into the throat. This is where the bleeding and swelling occur. Then the tube, a yard (metre) long, is run through the nasal passage, down the throat, into the stomach. Medicine or tonic is poured from a glass. Food is run through the tube. Choking and bleeding begin and last during the feedings. Tears stream from the corner of the eyes.

Source B: A suffragette poster of 1909, showing a prisoner being force-fed

Tasks

1. Study Source A. What can you learn from Source A about force-feeding?

2. How reliable are Sources A and B as evidence of force-feeding? Explain your answer using Sources A and B and your own knowledge.

The Conciliation Bill

The year 1910 seemed to offer a real chance of votes for women. Prime Minister Asquith set up a 'Conciliation Committee' of MPs from all parties, which drew up the Conciliation Bill. The bill gave the vote to all women who owned a house, part of a house or just a room. The only condition was that they must have complete control of the house. This meant that a husband and wife could not both vote if they lived in the same house.

The Conciliation Bill was supported by the WSPU, which suspended all militant action and held 4000 meetings to support it. However, the bill was delayed by the General Election of December 1910 and, in the following year, was dropped by Asquith who announced that he planned to introduce his own bill in favour of votes for women.

Emmeline and Christabel Pankhurst were infuriated by Asquith's actions and began a new wave of militancy, including window-smashing and arson (see page 9). Asquith was attacked several times by the suffragettes.

The Franchise and Registration Bill

In June 1912 Asquith introduced the Franchise and Registration Bill. It removed most of the remaining restrictions on the right to vote for males, including the household qualification. He planned to introduce an amendment to the bill that would include votes for women. However, the Speaker of the House of Commons rejected this amendment, insisting that giving women the vote would change the bill so much that it would have to be withdrawn.

Asquith's failure to keep his promise brought another wave of suffragette militancy, with attacks on the greens of golf courses (see page 9) and the burning down of derelict buildings. The orchid house and tea-rooms at Kew Gardens, in London, were wrecked. Suffragettes also managed to plant two bombs in a house belonging to Lloyd George, the Chancellor of the Exchequer, and destroyed part of it.

The 'Cat and Mouse Act'

More and more suffragettes were arrested, went on hunger strike and were force-fed. In 1913 the government introduced the Temporary Discharge Bill. Prisoners on hunger strike were released when very ill and sent back to prison when they had recovered. Emmeline Pankhurst went to prison twelve times in as many months and became very weak. This 'letting them go, then catching them again' led to the measure being nicknamed the 'Cat and Mouse Act'.

At first the new act appeared to solve the problem of hunger striking and avoided force-feeding. However, some suffragettes pretended to be ill in order to get themselves released. Once out of prison, they simply went back to their old ways and there was little that the government could do to stop them.

Source C: A 1914 suffragette poster

THE CAT AND MOUSE ACT
PASSED BY THE LIBERAL GOVERNMENT

THE LIBERAL CAT
ELECTORS VOTE AGAINST HIM!
KEEP THE LIBERAL OUT!

Tasks

3. *Study Source C. What was the purpose of this poster? Use details from the poster and your own knowledge to explain your answer.*

4. *Working in pairs:*
- *Which do you think was the more effective method of dealing with hunger striking – force-feeding or the 'Cat and Mouse Act'?*
- *Can you think of a more effective method?*

Why had women not been given the vote by 1914?

In 1914, on the eve of the First World War, and despite the activities of the three women's societies, women still did not have the vote. Reasons for this included people's reactions to suffragettes, the divisions in the women's movement, the attitude of the Liberal government and traditional male attitudes.

Reactions to suffragettes

The extreme actions of the suffragettes convinced many men, including members of the government and Parliament, that women were not sensible enough to deserve the vote. Prime Minister Asquith, especially, refused to give way to violent threats, as he thought this might encourage other groups to use the same methods.

Divisions in the women's movement

The campaign for the vote was weakened by differences between the three societies as well as divisions in the WSPU. Millicent Fawcett, leader of the NUWSS, often spoke of her admiration for the courage of the suffragettes. However, the wave of firebombs in 1912 and 1913 was too much for her. The WSPU became completely isolated from the actions of the other two societies.

Source A: **The Speaker of the House of Commons in 1913, writing in 1925**

The activities of the militant suffragettes had now (1913) reached the stage at which nothing was safe from their attacks. Churches were burnt, public buildings and private residences were destroyed, bombs were exploded, the police and individuals were assaulted, meetings broken up, and every imaginable device resorted to. The feeling in the House of Commons, caused by the lawless actions of the militants, hardened the opposition to their demands, with the result that on 6 May the Private Member's Bill, for which the Government had in the previous session promised support, was rejected on the second reading.

Source B: **From *My Own Story*, a book written by Emmeline Pankhurst in 1912**

What good did all this violent campaigning do us? We have often been asked that question. For one thing our campaign made woman's suffrage a matter of news – it had never been that before. Now the newspapers are full of us. The argument of politicians and the Suffragists has always been that once public opinion swings our way then without any force at all women will be given the vote. We agree that the public must be educated, but in 1906 there was a very large section of the public who were in favour of women's suffrage. But what good did that do? We called upon the government to give us the vote but they didn't. So, now we will fight for our cause.

Source C: **A comment by Lloyd George in 1913**

Haven't the suffragettes the sense to see that the very worst kind of campaigning for the vote is to try to intimidate or blackmail a man into giving them what he would otherwise gladly give?

Tasks

1. Study Source A. What can you learn from Source A about the activities of the suffragettes?

2. Study Sources A, B and C. Do Sources B and C support the views of Source A about the activities of the suffragettes? Explain your answer, using the sources.

Source D: An anti-suffragette postcard published in 1912

Source E: Millicent Fawcett, writing in 1911

The violence offered by the suffragettes has not been formidable, and the fiercest of the suffragettes have been far more ready to suffer pain than to inflict it. What those endured who underwent the hunger strike and the anguish of force-feeding can hardly be overestimated. Their courage made a deep impression on the public.

The WSPU was weakened by divisions and disagreements. One leading member, Emmeline Pethick-Lawrence, left the WSPU in 1912 due to the increased militancy and began to work on her own for votes for women. Sylvia Pankhurst also drifted away from the movement and spent more time working to improve the lives of the poor in the East End of London.

This left the WSPU in the hands of Emmeline and Christabel Pankhurst, who now directed the activities of the suffragettes. Emmeline took no notice of critics and simply called for more and more violence in the years before the outbreak of the First World War. This, in turn, made it more difficult for the Liberal government to introduce votes for women.

Attitude of Liberal governments

The Liberal governments of 1905–14 had numerous other issues to deal with before they were prepared to tackle votes for women. Indeed, votes for women was quite far down their list of priorities. Moreover, some leading Liberals, including Asquith, Prime Minister from 1908 onwards, were not keen on votes for women.

In the years 1905–11 they introduced a series of reforms to tackle the causes of poverty and ill-health in Britain (see Chapters 2 and 3). Furthermore, they had to deal with three other major problems in the years 1910–14:

- a clash between the House of Commons and the House of Lords which resulted, in 1911, in reform of the Lords
- the threat of civil war in Ireland over the issue of home rule (self-government)
- trade union unrest, which resulted in major strikes, including the Miners' Minimum Wage Strike of 1912.

Moreover, the actions of the suffragettes did much to upset leading Liberals such as Asquith and Lloyd George, who were frequently attacked by members of the WSPU.

Finally, the Liberal governments could not decide which women to give the vote to. They could not give the vote to all women because not all men had the vote. One possibility was to give it to women householders and the wives of householders. However, the Liberals feared that these women would vote mainly for the Conservatives. To the WSPU it looked as though the Liberals were simply stalling for time. In fact, the Liberals knew that the majority of voters in Britain did not regard votes for women as an important issue.

Traditional male attitude

Furthermore, many men continued to believe that a woman's place was in the home. Giving women the vote and getting them involved in politics would distract them from their domestic role.

Tasks

3. Study Source D and use your own knowledge. Why do you think this was so widely publicised?

4. How successful were the methods used by the three different women's societies? Make a copy of the following grid and give a rating out of 10 for each society. Some points have been included for you.

Society	Strengths	Weaknesses	Rating out of 10
NUWSS		Methods were too slow.	
WFL	Publicity, especially refusing to do census		
WSPU			

5. 'The main reason women did not have the vote by 1914 was the actions of the suffragettes.'

How far do Sources A–F support this statement? Use details from the sources and your own knowledge to explain your answer.

6. Study Source G. Think of a suitable headline.

Examination practice

This section provides guidance on how to answer Question 1 on Paper 3, which is worth six marks.

Question 1 – inference

Study Source A. What can you learn from Source A about Millicent Fawcett's attitude to the militancy of 1908?

> **Source A: Millicent Fawcett writing in 1908 about the arrest of suffragettes by the authorities and their subsequent hunger striking**
>
> *Militancy is hated by me, and the majority of suffragists. None of the triumphs of the women's movement have been won by physical force. They have been triumphs of moral and spiritual force. But militancy has been brought into existence by the blind blundering of politicians. If men had been treated by the House of Commons as women have been treated, there would have been bloody reprisals all over the country.*

The source suggests that Millicent Fawcett is against the extreme methods of the suffragettes.

She insists that any past gains for women's rights have not been achieved by physical force.

Source A
Millicent Fawcett writing in 1908 about the arrest of suffragettes by the authorities and their subsequent hunger striking Militancy is hated by me, and the majority of suffragists. None of the triumphs of the women's movement have been won by physical force. They have been triumphs of moral and spiritual force. But militancy has been brought into existence by the blind blundering of politicians. If men had been treated by the House of Commons as women have been treated, there would have been bloody reprisals all over the country.

She also blames the politicians for the extreme methods used by the suffragettes.

She justifies this by mentioning the blind blundering of politicians.

How to answer

- You are being asked to read between the lines of a source to make inferences about what it tells you about what the question asks – in question 1 this would be attitudes to militancy.
- To do well in this question, you must **support** your inferences. To do this, you need to quote words or phrases from the source (or details from the picture if it is a visual source).
- Begin your answer with 'Source … suggests that …' In this way you will make a judgement and avoid repeating the contents of the source.
- Look for key words in the source that you can use to make inferences. You could tackle this by highlighting the different points the source makes (as in the example above right).
- You need to make at least two supported inferences (there are four examples for Source A above right).

Now have a go yourself

Try answering this question using the steps shown above.

Study Source B. What can you learn from Source B about attitudes to votes for women?

> **Source B: From a speech by Frederick Ryland, an MP, in 1896**
>
> *Why should a person otherwise qualified be refused a vote simply on the grounds of sex? Mrs B's gardener or coachman will probably have a vote, while she is without one.*

Children's welfare measures and old age pensions

Source A: From *People of the Abyss* by Jack London, an American writer, 1903

Nowhere in the streets of London may one escape the sight of abject poverty, while five minutes' walk from almost any point will bring one to a slum; but the region my hansom was now penetrating was one unending slum. The streets were filled with a new and different race of people, short of stature, and of wretched or beer-sodden appearance. Here and there lurched a drunken man or woman, and the air was obscene with sounds of jangling and squabbling. At a market, tottery old men and women were searching in the garbage thrown in the mud for rotten potatoes, beans, and vegetables, while little children clustered like flies around a festering mass of fruit, thrusting their arms to the shoulders into the liquid corruption, and drawing forth morsels ... which they devoured on the spot.

Task

Study Source A. What can you learn from Source A about the city of London in 1903?

At the beginning of the twentieth century, Britain was the richest and most powerful nation in the world. The wealth of the country was clearly visible when visitors looked at the remarkable buildings and homes of the rich in Britain's cities. However, if they took the trouble, they could also see widespread poverty both in the cities and the rural areas. The reports of Booth and Rowntree showed the extent of deprivation, and the poor health of the recruits for the Boer War (1899–1902) made some politicians realise that reforms were needed. Some saw reforms as a necessary humanitarian reaction and others saw them as economically crucial if Britain was to compete with countries such as the USA and Germany. The first reforms dealt with young children and then, in 1908, Old Age Pensions were introduced.

This chapter answers the following questions:

• Why were reforms introduced to help children and the old?
• What were the key features of the reforms for children?
• What were the key features of the Old Age Pensions Act?

Examination skills

In this chapter you will be given guidance on how to answer the question analysing representations, Question 2, which is worth eight marks.

Why were reforms introduced to help children and the old?

Source A: Photograph of slum children in York, 1900

Source B: From *Poverty: A Study of Town Life*, 1901 by Seebohm Rowntree

*The poor must never purchase a halfpenny newspaper or spend a penny to buy a ticket for a popular concert. They cannot save, nor can they join a sick club or a **Trade Union**, because they cannot afford the contributions. The children must have no pocket money for dolls, marbles or sweets. The mother must never buy any pretty clothes for herself or her children. The wage earner must never be absent from his work for a single day.*

In 1900, despite the wealth of Britain, there were huge numbers of poor people. The extent of the problem of poverty was highlighted in the reports of Charles Booth and Seebohm Rowntree. Booth was a businessman from Liverpool and Rowntree was a Quaker industrialist and sociologist from York. Both had a keen interest in the lives of the ordinary people of Britain.

Booth conducted a survey into poverty in London and published his findings in a report called *Life and Labour of the People in London*. The report contained several volumes and was published over a period of twelve years (1891–1903). Rowntree's report *Poverty: A Study of Town Life* (1901) looked at poverty in York.

Both reports came up with similar findings. Booth showed that 31 per cent of Londoners lived below what he called the 'poverty line', by which he meant that they did not have enough money to buy food, clothes and shelter.

In his study, Rowntree said that there were two types of poverty – primary and secondary. Primary poverty, he argued, was where the family would never earn enough money to provide the necessities of life. Families suffering from secondary poverty had just enough but did not have anything left over for emergencies, such as medical treatment. Rowntree indicated that about 30 per cent of York's population was living in these two states of poverty.

If families were unable to cope they had to rely on charity. In 1905, there were about 700 private charities which tried to help the poor. For example, it was common for poor parents to abandon their children and Dr Barnardo's charity was established to look after these destitute children. The Barnardo's charity helped thousands of children. The **Salvation Army** had been founded towards the end of the nineteenth century and had become active in helping the poor in London.

The last resort for families was the **workhouse**. Workhouses had been established to help the very poor but conditions inside them were extremely harsh. The sexes were kept separate, families were split up, the discipline was strict and the work provided was hard and monotonous. Many people were frightened to enter the workhouse and would do almost anything to avoid doing so.

Source C: Dinner time at Marylebone workhouse, 1900

Source E: *Efficiency and Empire*, by Arnold White, a journalist, 1901

In the Manchester district, 11,000 men offered themselves for war service between the outbreak of hostilities in October 1899 and July 1900. Of this number 8000 were found to be physically unfit to carry a rifle and stand the fatigues of discipline. Of the 3000 who were accepted only 1200 attained the moderate standard of muscular power and chest measurement required by the military authorities.

Source D: From an interview with 80-year-old Ada Haigh, in 1975, explaining why she did not want to go into the local hospital that year

I didn't want to go to the hospital because it used to be the workhouse. I remember it as the workhouse. My grandma had had to go in there and she died there. She got a pauper's burial. I nearly had to go in when my dad was out of a job for three months but my mother took in extra washing and I had to help her and I missed school. My mother kept saying we had to stay out of the workhouse because people would call us names and we'd be the lowest of the low in the village. I knew that it was a horrible place, the rules were horrible and as far as I'm concerned it will always be the horrible workhouse.

Tasks

1. Study Sources A, B and C. How far do these sources agree about poverty in Britain at the beginning of the twentieth century? Explain your answer, using the sources.

2. Briefly explain why the reports of Booth and Rowntree were important.

3. How reliable are Sources C and D as evidence of the workhouse? Explain your answer, using the sources.

4. Can you suggest reasons why conditions in the workhouse were so harsh?

5. Study Source E. What can you learn from Source E about health in Britain in 1900?

In addition, the Boer War showed politicians that poverty had far-reaching consequences. As many as two out of three recruits failed the army medical test (see Source E). The politicians realised that Britain needed a healthy population to maintain its Empire and to compete with the rising powers of Germany and the USA.

What were the key features of the reforms for children?

Children waiting outside a hall for free school dinners in London's East End, 1912

School meals

Following the victory of the Liberal Party in the 1906 General Election, there was a commitment from the new government to bring in some social reforms. Some of the younger members of the so-called **New Liberals**, such as Lloyd George and Winston Churchill, wanted to introduce legislation which would help the most vulnerable in society – the young and the old.

Throughout the 1880s and 1890s there were reports which showed that hungry children could not and did not learn at school. The first piece of legislation, the Provision of School Meals Act (1906), was introduced as a bill by a Labour MP. This act permitted local authorities to provide free school meals. By 1914, 158,000 children were receiving free meals. However, the law was permissive. That is, it did not force local councils to provide meals and about half the councils in Britain did not provide them. Some said it was because they would have had to raise the local rates and this would have proved unpopular.

> **Source A: From a pamphlet written during the 1885 London School Board elections**
>
> *I support one good free meal a day. As all unbiased medical opinions declare that it is impossible to educate half-starved or insufficiently fed children without physical and mental injury, and under our present system of society it is impossible for our working classes to ensure their children proper nourishment.*

Medical legislation

Further attempts to safeguard the health of children came in 1907 with the Notification of Births Act. By this act, parents had to inform the local Medical Officer of Health when a child was born. The Officer could then arrange for a trained health visitor to call on the mother at her home and teach her how to protect the baby's health. This act was introduced because there was a growing awareness of the high death rate of children under five and especially the death rate of children in their first year, known as the **infant mortality** rate.

In 1907, the Liberals introduced the Education (Administrative Provisions) Act. This act introduced a schools medical service and children were to be medically inspected on a regular basis. The inspections were free, but parents had to pay for any treatment that might follow. However, in 1912, school clinics were set up to provide some free treatment for those parents who could not afford it.

Children's Charter, 1908

The Children's Act of 1908 (also known as Children and Young Persons Act and more commonly The Children's Charter) introduced a series of measures designed to protect young people.

In 1900, the law treated children in the same ways as adults and if found guilty of a crime they would be sent to adult prisons. Children could smoke and drink alcohol and large numbers of them had part-time jobs or helped out at home, making things for sale such as brushes and matchboxes. The aim of the act was to protect children and, for the first time, it defined the age limit of childhood as 14.

Key features of the Children's Charter

- Parents could be prosecuted for any acts of cruelty and neglect towards their children.
- Parents could no longer insure their children's lives.
- It was illegal to send children begging.
- It was illegal to sell children under 16 tobacco, alcohol and fireworks.
- Children under 14 were not allowed into pubs.
- Children under 14 who had broken the law could not be sent to adult prisons.
- Special juvenile courts were established to try those children accused of crimes.
- Those children found guilty of committing crimes were sent to Borstals – specially designed custodial centres for the young.
- Children were prevented from working in dangerous trades such as chain and box manufacturing.
- All children's homes had to be registered and were subject to regular inspection.
- The act introduced the registration of foster parents.
- Local authorities were granted powers to keep poor children out of the workhouse and protect them from abuse.

Tasks

1. Study Source A. What can you learn from Source A about the need to provide meals for children at school?

2. Working in pairs, present a case supporting the statement: 'The School Meals Act was more important than Medical Legislation'.

3. Study the terms of the Children's Charter. What picture does the act give of the life of some children at this time?

4. Choose three points from the Children's Charter and explain why you consider them to be the most important of the act.

What were the key features of the Old Age Pensions Act?

Source A: One of the first people to receive an Old Age Pension, *Daily Record*, 9 January 1909

1908 Old Age Pensions Act

- To qualify for the pension, a person had to have reached the age of 70, and be a British subject who had resided in the United Kingdom for 20 years.
- A single person would receive 5 shillings (25p) and a married couple 7s 6d (37.5p).
- The pension was paid on a sliding scale based on earnings and if a person earned less than £21 per year (p/a) then s/he was entitled to the full pension.

The scale was as follows:

£21 to £23 12s 6d p/a	Rate of Pension 4s (20p) p/week.
£23 12s 6d to £26 5s p/a	Rate of Pension 3s (15p) p/week.
£26 5s to £28 17s 6d p/a	Rate of Pension 2s (10p) p/week.
£28 17s 6d to £31 10s p/a	Rate of Pension 1s (5p) p/week.

If a person earned more than £31 10s in a year then they would not receive a pension.

The following categories of people were not eligible for the pension. Those who:
- had been convicted of an offence involving imprisonment
- had habitually failed to work according to their ability, opportunity and need
- had been in receipt of help from the Poor Law (money or workhouse) since 1 January 1908
- had been convicted for being drunk under the Inebriates Act of 1898
- were detained in a lunatic asylum.

At the beginning of the twentieth century, when working-class people became too old to work, they had to rely on their own savings (if they had any), or help from charities or their families or be prepared to enter the workhouse. Following their political beliefs, the New Liberals in the government wanted to help this section of society and began to plan the introduction of a state pension.

The Old Age Pensions Act was passed by the Liberals in 1908 and it was hailed as a tremendous reform. Lloyd George, as Chancellor of the Exchequer, had to raise taxes in order to pay for the pensions because the payment was non-contributory. That is, those who received the pension did not have to pay into a fund; they were given it as of right.

Lloyd George stated that part of his motive in introducing pensions was to 'lift the shadow of the workhouse from the homes of the poor'. It was estimated that pensions would cost the government £16 million per year. More than 600,000 people were eligible for the pension when it was first paid in 1909. For many old people, the pension removed the fear that they would have to enter the workhouse. By 1914, almost one million people were receiving the pension.

The Liberals, votes for women and social reform

Source B: An extract from Lloyd George's budget speech of 1909, which raised taxes to pay for old age pensions announced in 1908

This is a war Budget. It is for raising money to wage implacable warfare against poverty and squalor. I cannot help hoping and believing that before this generation has passed away, we shall have advanced a great step towards that good time, when poverty, and the wretchedness and human degradation which always follows in its camp, will be as remote to the people of this country as the wolves which once infested its forests.

Source C: A cartoon published in the magazine *Punch*, 5 August 1908

THE PHILANTHROPIC HIGHWAYMAN.

Mr. Lloyd-George. *"I'LL MAKE 'EM PITY THE AGED POOR!"*

Source D: An account of old people drawing their first pension, from *Lark Rise to Candleford*, a memoir by Flora Thompson

At first when they went to the Post Office ... tears of gratitude would run down the cheeks of some, and they would say as they picked up their money, 'God bless that Lord George!' ... and 'God bless you, Miss!' and there were flowers from their gardens and apples from their trees for the girl who merely handed them the money.

Tasks

1. What does Source A tell us about the introduction of old age pensions?

2. How reliable are Sources B and D as evidence of old age pensions? Explain your answer using Sources B and D and your own knowledge.

3. Study Source C and use your own knowledge. What was the purpose of this cartoon? Use details from the cartoon and your own knowledge to explain your answer.

4. Study the categories of people who were not eligible for the pension. What does this tell you about Britain at this time?

5. Copy the tables below. Construct a balance sheet of the reforms for the young and the old, showing the improvements and limitations of the reforms. Some points have been included for you.

Young	Improvements	Limitations
	Free meals	Local authorities not compelled to provide them

Old	Improvements	Limitations
	Pension	Began at 70

Examination practice

This section provides guidance on how to answer Question 2 on Paper 3, which is worth eight marks.

Question 2 – analysing representations

Study Source A and use your own knowledge. What was the purpose of this representation? Use details from the representation and your own knowledge to explain your answer.

How to answer

A **representation** is usually a poster, or a painting, designed with a 'message'. You have to use your skills of **inference** (see Question 1, page 16) and your own knowledge to explain what the **purpose** of this message is and how it is put across. In order to do this you need to:

- Start by examining the representation carefully so that you will be able to use details from it to back up your answer.
- While you are examining the representation, draw inferences from it. What is it suggesting?

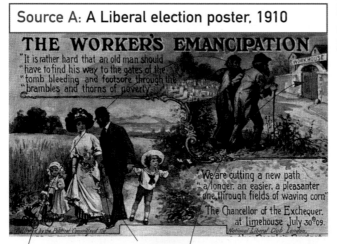

Source A: A Liberal election poster, 1910

What is its tone or attitude? What is the overall message?

- Start your answer by explaining the purpose of the representation. This is the most important skill which, if carried out successfully, will lead to higher level marks. In other words what is the poster trying to make people think? Is it trying to get people to support or oppose a person or event? Use details from the source to back up your answer.
- Support your answer on the purpose of the source with your own contextual knowledge – in other words, your knowledge of what was going on at that time. For example, in this case you can explain about some or all of the following:
  - attitudes to the poor at this time
  - the role of Lloyd George
  - Liberal reforms helping the weak in society.

To get top marks you have to say something from your own knowledge about the context, that is the history surrounding the source.

To plan an answer to this question, you could annotate the source as shown in the example below. Part of an answer showing how to support the inferences from the source with contextual knowledge is also given below.

Purpose
To turn people against the Tory Party by showing them as greedy and encouraging support for Lloyd George by showing him as generous.

Inference
The poster suggests that life will be easier and workers will be freed (emancipated) from the fear of ending life in a workhouse.

Own knowledge
The Liberal Party campaigned in the 1910 election for a People's Budget, bringing in Old Age Pensions and Unemployment Benefit.

Overall message
Vote Liberal in order to help the old and create a fairer society in which the wealthy can help the poor.

Source A is an election poster and was published to win votes for the Liberals. Hence it seeks to show that the Liberals are a caring and thoughtful group of politicians who care for workers when they grow old. The poster clearly puts over the message that a vote for them will help people. It also suggests that there were rich people who could afford to pay higher taxes to help finance the Old Age Pension. The poster also aimed to show how the Liberals wanted to create a fairer society and to explain that there were some rich people who opposed the Old Age Pension.

Labour Exchanges and the National Insurance Act

Source A: Liberal Party poster promoting National Insurance, 1911

THE DAWN OF HOPE.

Mr. LLOYD GEORGE'S National Health Insurance Bill provides for the insurance of the Worker in case of Sickness.

Support the Liberal Government
in their policy of
SOCIAL REFORM.

Task

What does Source A tell us about the Liberals and National Insurance?

After the success of reforms with children and old age pensions, the Liberal Party moved its emphasis to the workers. The Liberals hoped to tackle poverty by helping workers who were unemployed and those who experienced sickness. There was much concern, not only from workers but also from doctors and savings organisations, when the plans for a National Insurance scheme were published. However, by 1914, the Liberals had introduced Labour Exchanges and had a National Insurance scheme that covered millions of workers in the event of illness and unemployment.

This chapter answers the following questions:

• What were Labour Exchanges and why were they set up?
• Why was the National Insurance Act introduced?
• What were the key features of the National Insurance scheme?

What were Labour Exchanges and why were they set up?

Camberwell Green Labour Exchange, 1910

As part of its policy to help workers, the Liberal government tried to help the unemployed. Workers had to search for jobs themselves and this was time consuming and wasteful. The Liberals therefore introduced Labour Exchanges, which would bring together people looking for work and employers looking for workers.

Winston Churchill, President of the Board of Trade, was in charge of this reform and 83 exchanges were opened in February 1910. By 1914, there were 450 and more than one million people had registered. William Beveridge was put in charge of the day-to-day running of the exchanges and his experiences of working with unemployed people enabled him to advise Lloyd George about the National Insurance scheme (see page 28).

The first Labour Exchanges had separate entrances and rooms for men and women and different rooms for skilled and unskilled workmen. 'Juveniles' as young as twelve years old queued up to find work.

Task

Explain why the establishment of Labour Exchanges assisted working people.

Why was the National Insurance Act introduced?

As part of their drive to help workers, the Liberals wanted to help those workers who became ill or unemployed. Some workers did try to provide for such eventualities by taking out insurance policies or saving with Friendly Societies. Most workers were unable to afford private schemes.

The Liberals recognised that the government had to help its citizens on **humanitarian** grounds but also needed to ensure that its workers would not slip into a spiral of poverty, which could lead to Britain not being able to compete as an **industrial nation**. The act allowed many British workers to avoid relying on the **Poor Law** and prevented them from slipping into abject poverty. Workers objected to money being taken directly out of their wages and the government used the slogan 'ninepence for fourpence' to try to convince them that they were contributing to a worthwhile scheme.

The National Insurance Act (1911) was in two parts. The first dealt with health and the second with unemployment (see boxes below).

One aspect which caused uproar was that domestic servants were covered by National Insurance. The servants themselves were unhappy at being forced to pay contributions out of their very low wages. Employers (usually the woman of the house, or the mistress) were also outraged and some were arrested for refusing to pay (see Source D on page 29).

National Insurance Act (Health)

- All workers between sixteen and seventy who earned up to £160 had to join.
- The workers had to contribute 4d per week (directly from their wages), while employers paid 3d and the state 2d.
- Workers were entitled to free medical care and advice from a general practitioner.
- Medical benefit of 10s (50p) per week for 13 weeks and then 5s (25p) for the following 13 weeks.
- Disability benefit of 5s (25p) per week.
- Maternity benefit of 30s (£1.50) on the birth of the child.
- The right to treatment of tuberculosis (TB) in a **sanatorium**.

National Insurance Act (Unemployment)

- It dealt with those industries that experienced particular problems or cyclical/seasonal employment such as engineering, building, iron-founding, shipbuilding, saw-milling (in total about 2.5 million workers).
- Workers contributed 2½d (1p), employers 2½d (1p) and the state 1.66d (0.7p).
- Workers were to receive 7 shillings (35p) per week for up to 15 weeks per year in the event of unemployment.
- Benefits were paid at the Labour Exchange.
- The worker received a stamp on his insurance card to prove his eligibility for benefits.

What were the key features of the National Insurance scheme?

By 1913, 2.3 million people were insured under the scheme for unemployment benefit. There were almost 15 million people insured for sickness benefit, including about 4 million women. For many years after the passing of the act, workers who were off work would say they were 'on the Lloyd George'.

Source A: From a speech by Prime Minister Asquith, the Albert Hall, London, December 1909

Sickness, invalidity, unemployment – these are the spectres which are always hovering on the horizon of possibility, I may also say of certainty, to the industrious workman. We believe here also the time has come for the State to lend a helping hand. That is the secret, or at least one of the secrets, of the Budget this year. It was a Budget which sought by taxes on the accumulations of the rich and luxuries of the well-to-do to provide the sinews of war for the initiation and the prosecution of what must be a long, a costly, social campaign.

Source B: From Lloyd George's speech about National Insurance in the House of Commons, 4 May 1911

What is the explanation that only a portion of the working classes has made provision against sickness and unemployment? Very few can afford to pay the premiums, and pay them continuously. You need to pay 1s 6d [7.5p] or 2s [10p] per week at the lowest. During a period of unemployment, when workers are earning nothing, they cannot pay the premiums. That is the reason why less than one half of the workers in this country have made provision for sickness and one tenth for unemployment.

Source C: A postcard printed in 1911 to mark the introduction of the National Insurance scheme

THIS STAMP WILL TAKE A BIT OF LICKING

" Reg. and Copyright applied for

Source D: A cartoon about the National Insurance Act, *Daily Mirror*, 23 November 1911

WE PROPOSE TAXING THESE —

IN ORDER TO KEEP THESE

Source F: From a report in the *Daily Telegraph* of a speech made by Lloyd George, 2 February 1912

You have, I suppose, in England, twelve or thirteen millions of insured persons. Had I not believed that this Act of Parliament was going to relieve a large amount of undeserved suffering, I would not have touched it (hear, hear). I felt that it was worth incurring all the trouble and all the labour, worth facing all the misrepresentations and all the malignant abuse, for the purpose of putting it through, and when, at the end of a few years, you and I will realise the amount of distress that we have saved we shall be able, at any rate, to share in the satisfaction which will be deep and permanent in your lives and in mine (loud cheers).

Tasks

1. *Study Source A. What can you learn from Source A about the reasons for the introduction of National Insurance?*

2. *What can you learn from Source B about the workers' provision against sickness and unemployment?*

3. *How reliable is Source C as evidence of the National Insurance scheme?*

4. *Study Source D. What was the purpose of this cartoon? Use details from the cartoon and your own knowledge to explain your answer.*

5. *How reliable are Sources E and F as evidence of the National Insurance scheme? Explain your answer using Sources E and F and your own knowledge.*

Source E: From a speech by Winston Churchill, 1911

National Insurance is the most decisive step yet taken upon the path of social organisation. The cruel waste of disease and unemployment, breaking down men and women, breaking up homes and families, will for the first time be countered by the whole strength of the nation.

Key Topic 2: The part played by the British on the Western Front

Task

What can you learn from Source A about the Western Front?

This key topic examines the part played by the British armies on the Western Front during the First World War (1914–18). Within a few weeks of the outbreak of war, the **British Expeditionary Force (BEF)** had landed in France and played an important role in the failure of the German Schlieffen Plan and the subsequent race for the Channel ports. This was followed by over three years of trench warfare on the Western Front, with neither side able to break through. British armies made a major contribution to this trench warfare, more especially during the Somme offensive of 1916. Moreover, the British commander Sir Douglas Haig and British forces played a vital role in the events of 1918, which culminated in the defeat of Germany.

Each chapter explains a key issue and examines important lines of enquiry as outlined below.

Chapter 4 The BEF and 1914 (pages 31–40)
- What was the Schlieffen Plan?
- Why did the Schlieffen Plan fail?
- Why was there a race for the sea?
- What was the situation by 1914?

Chapter 5 Britain's contribution to the Western Front 1915–17 (pages 41–54)
- What was the nature of trench warfare?
- Why was there a stalemate on the Western Front?
- What part did Haig play in the stalemate?

- Why was there no breakthrough at the Somme?
- How were new methods of warfare used on the Western Front?

Chapter 6 The end of the war (pages 55–61)
- Why did the Spring Offensive of 1918 fail?
- What part did the British play in the drive to victory?
- How and why did Germany collapse in 1918?

The BEF and 1914

Source A: An August 1914 German newspaper illustration showing the German army attacking the fortress of Liège

Task

Study Source A and use your own knowledge. What was the purpose of this illustration? Use details from the illustration and your own knowledge to explain your answer.

As soon as war broke out in early August 1914, the Germans launched the Schlieffen Plan, by which they intended to quickly defeat France in the west, within three or four weeks, before concentrating on Russia in the east. The failure of the plan led to a race for the sea between Britain and Germany, culminating in the First Battle of Ypres, which stopped the German advance. In November 1914 both sides dug themselves in for the winter. These trenches were to last for over three years.

This chapter answers the following questions:

- What was the Schlieffen Plan?
- Why did the Schlieffen Plan fail?
- Why was there a race for the sea?
- What was the situation by the end of 1914?

Examination skills

In this chapter you will be given guidance on how to answer the question using a source and your own knowledge, Question 3, which is worth ten marks.

What was the Schlieffen Plan?

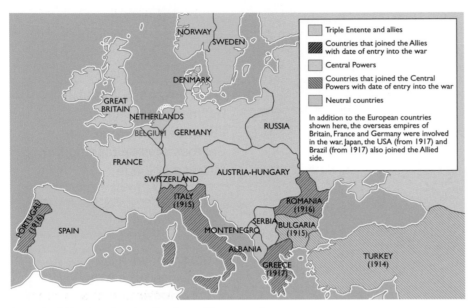

A map of Europe showing the two alliance systems

The First World War was fought between the **Central Powers**, Germany and Austria-Hungary, and the **Triple Entente** of Britain, France and Russia (the Allies).

The Central Powers

Of all the Great Powers, Germany had the largest peacetime army of over two million men, which was well trained, organised and disciplined. Germany was also the only power with a plan to fight the war. Its weakness was its ally, Austria-Hungary, which had an army of less than one million men, many of whom were non-Austrians from the Austrian Empire and not keen to fight in the war.

The Triple Entente

Britain was the only country among the Great Powers which did not have **conscription**. It had a small, professional army of about 700,000 men. In the years before the outbreak of war a British Expeditionary Force (BEF) was assembled, which could be quickly transported to France.

France had an army of 1.25 million men but it lacked the organisation and efficiency of its German counterpart and had no real plan, apart from invading Alsace-Lorraine. Russia also had an army of 1.25 million men but it was poorly equipped, with generally incompetent commanders.

The Schlieffen Plan

Germany had long feared a war on two fronts, with France to the west and Russia to the east. In 1905 Count von Schlieffen, the Chief of the German General Staff, prepared a plan to avoid having to fight on both fronts at the same time. He believed that, due to the terrible state of its roads and its inefficient railways, Russia would take about six weeks to mobilise. In the meantime the German armies would quickly knock France out of the war before dealing with Russia.

How could they defeat the French in less than six weeks? The border with France was too strong to attack – it was protected by strong French fortresses as well as a great number of troops. Nevertheless, there was one gap in the French defences – the Belgian frontier. Belgium, however, was a neutral country whose neutrality was guaranteed by the Great Powers, including Britain. Despite this, von Schlieffen decided to attack through Belgium. The Belgian army was small and would easily be brushed aside. While the main French armies attacked through Alsace-Lorraine, the German armies would sweep through Belgium and into northern France. The French would realise their mistake too late, by which time Paris would have been taken and the French armies

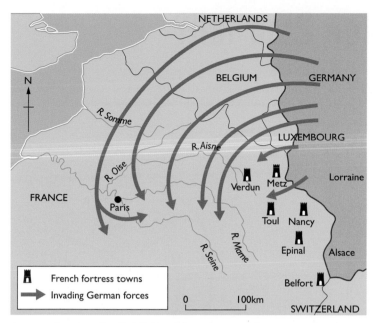

A map showing the Schlieffen Plan, Germany's strategy for the invasion of France

What did it need to succeed?

The Schlieffen Plan made several assumptions.

- The Belgians would not resist; or, if they did, they would be easily defeated and the German armies would quickly advance through the country.
- The French would attack through Alsace-Lorraine and would be too slow to realise their mistake or understand the German plan.
- Russia would take at least six weeks to mobilise and at first Germany would only need to send a small force to the east.
- The British Expeditionary Force (BEF) would arrive too late to stop the German advance.

would be surrounded. With the fall of the French capital, all French enthusiasm for the war would collapse and their armies would surrender.

Schlieffen realised that the invasion of Belgium would force Britain into the war but believed that France would be defeated before the British armed forces could make any impact.

Source A: A British cartoon, early August 1914

Tasks

1. *Study Source A. Why was this cartoon published so widely? Use details from the cartoon and your own knowledge to explain your answer.*

2. *Complete the flow diagram below to show the various stages of the Schlieffen Plan.*

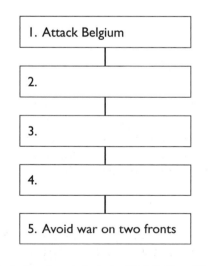

| 1. Attack Belgium |
| 2. |
| 3. |
| 4. |
| 5. Avoid war on two fronts |

3. *Look at what the Schlieffen Plan needed to succeed. What do you think could go wrong?*

Why did the Schlieffen Plan fail?

Belgian resistance

The Belgians, using their forts, resisted and slowed down the German advance. On 3 August an army of over one million Germans marched into Belgium. Deep concrete forts protecting Antwerp, Liège and Namur delayed the Germans. Heavy guns had to be brought up to pound the defences to rubble. Antwerp did not surrender until October. Belgian resistance gave the BEF time to arrive.

Source A: A photograph of Belgian troops guarding a bridge over a railway at Termonde, September 1914

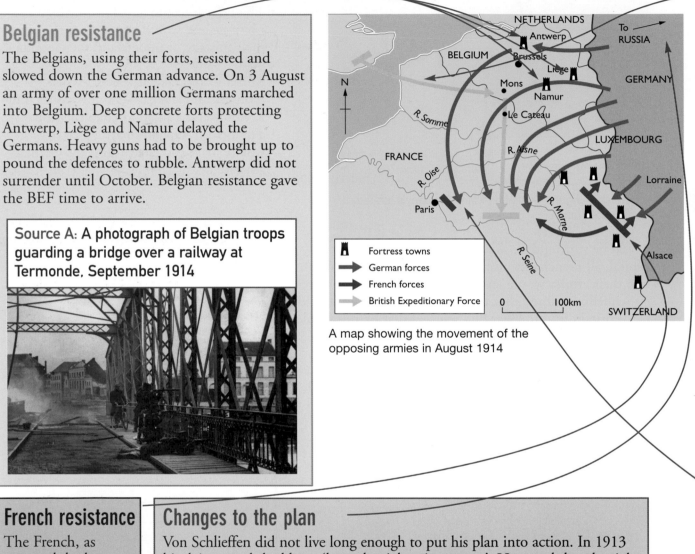

A map showing the movement of the opposing armies in August 1914

Map labels: NETHERLANDS, To RUSSIA, Antwerp, BELGIUM, Brussels, Liège, GERMANY, Mons, Namur, R. Somme, Le Cateau, R. Aisne, LUXEMBOURG, FRANCE, R. Oise, Lorraine, R. Marne, Paris, R. Seine, Alsace, SWITZERLAND

Key:
- Fortress towns
- German forces
- French forces
- British Expeditionary Force

0   100km

French resistance

The French, as expected, had attacked Alsace-Lorraine and had suffered heavy casualties. The delays achieved by the Belgians and British gave the French time to move their troops towards Paris and make a stand on the Marne (see page 36).

Changes to the plan

Von Schlieffen did not live long enough to put his plan into action. In 1913 his dying words had been 'keep the right wing strong'. He urged that the right wing of the German army should be six times stronger than any other. The new German commander, von Moltke, ignored this advice and the army was not strong enough to carry out the plan. The German armies that invaded Belgium were 100,000 soldiers short because von Moltke sent additional forces to reinforce the Russian front.

Von Moltke made other crucial changes to the original plan. Schlieffen wanted a wide sweep through the Netherlands, Luxembourg and Belgium. This was changed to a narrower attack through Belgium and Luxembourg. In addition German armies were supposed to encircle Paris. This plan was abandoned in early September and they moved to the east, leading to the Battle of the Marne (see page 36).

The BEF

The Kaiser had dismissed the BEF as a 'contemptible little army'. However the BEF, under the command of Sir John French, started to arrive in France on 18 August, much more quickly than the Germans had expected. It was a small but excellently trained force. The new German commander, von Moltke, had to transfer troops from the Eastern Front to face the BEF.

On 23 August the BEF stumbled into the Germans near the mining town of Mons. The BEF were heavily outnumbered and had to retreat. They had, however, further delayed the German advance. Three days later there was a battle at Le Cateau. Again the British retreated but the Germans were slowed down.

Source B: From a German soldier about the Battle of Mons

From now on matters went from bad to worse. Wherever I looked, right or left, there were dead or wounded, quivering in convulsions, groaning terribly, blood oozing from flesh wounds. We had to go back. A bad defeat, there could be no denying it. In our first battle we had been badly beaten, and by the English – by the English we had so laughed at a few hours before.

German exhaustion

The advance through Belgium and into northern France took its toll on the German soldiers.

Source D: The diary entry of a German officer, September 1914

Our soldiers stagger forward, their faces coated with dust, their uniforms in rags. They look like living scarecrows.

Source C: An official British painting of 1914 of the charge of the British 9th Lancers at Mons, by Richard Caton Woodville II

Tasks

1. *Source A is an official Belgian photograph. Devise a caption for the photograph that could have been used by the Belgian government.*

2. *Study Source B. What can you learn from Source B about the battle of Mons?*

3. *How reliable are Sources B and C as evidence of the events of 1914? Explain your answer using Sources B and C and your own knowledge. (For guidance on answering this type of question, see page 80.)*

4. *How important were each of the following countries in the failure of the Schlieffen Plan? Make a copy of the table and give each a rating with a brief explanation.*

	Decisive	Important	Unimportant
Belgium			
Britain			
France			
Germany			

5. *Source D is the diary entry of a German officer for 2 September. Write possible entries in his diary for 3 and 23 August.*

The Battle of the Marne

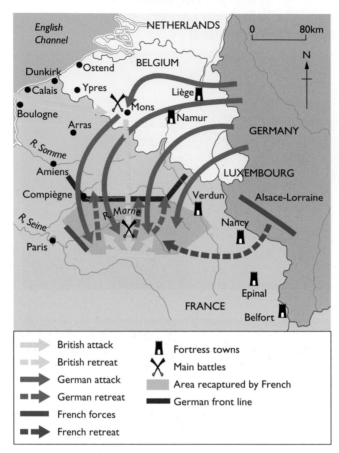

A map showing the Battle of the Marne, September 1914

By 5 September 1914 the German armies had reached the River Marne, just 65 kilometres to the north-east of Paris. Many Parisians grabbed what belongings they could and fled the city. However, instead of moving to the west of Paris, as in the original plan, the German armies moved to the east. In addition, the two German armies that had advanced furthest, under Generals von Kluck and von Bulow, had split and a gap had appeared.

The French meanwhile had quickly moved their armies from Alsace-Lorraine eastwards to the Marne to protect Paris. Their armies were further reinforced with every available soldier from Paris, transported by taxis and buses. Between the French armies and the Germans stood the BEF, pushed back from Belgium but still intact.

British **reconnaissance balloons** spotted the gap between the two German armies. Cautiously at first, the BEF advanced into the gap, supported by the French. Initially the Germans resisted and held their ground. The ensuing battle lasted for over a week across a front of 200 kilometres. Finally, in order to close the gap, the exhausted German armies fell back to a safe position 60 kilometres north of the River Aisne.

Source E: A French soldier remembers the Marne

The wounded cry out. One of them begged the Colonel first to help him, then to finish him off. Finally the Colonel ordered an advance. 'Let's go boys, we must move forward. Your comrades are out there. You can't leave them alone.'

The Battle of the Marne was the only decisive battle on the Western Front until 1918:
• It signalled the final failure of the Schlieffen Plan
• The Germans reverted to Plan B, the race for the Channel ports.

Tasks

6. Study Source E. What can you learn from Source E about the French troops at the Marne?

7. Imagine you are a military adviser to von Moltke in 1914. What changes would you suggest to ensure that the Schlieffen Plan succeeds?

Why was there a race for the sea?

The Germans now tried a new plan, which was to **outflank** the British. They hoped to reach the English Channel and seize the ports. This would cut off the BEF's retreat and prevent further British reinforcements. The BEF, however, also advanced north and there began a 'race for the sea'. The British arrived on the Belgian coast in time, helped by the Belgians who deliberately flooded their countryside, just as the Germans tried one last time to curve round northwards behind the Allies.

The first battle of Ypres, October 1914

When the British reached the sea, they sought to defend the Channel ports. In hastily dug trench positions they made their stand at the Belgian town of Ypres, which they nicknamed 'Wipers'.

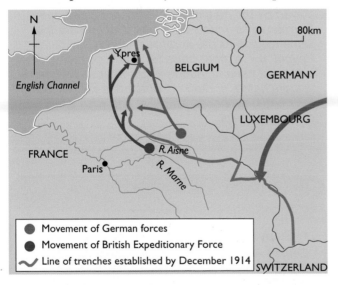

A map showing the 'race for the sea'

Source A: British troops arriving in the market place at Ypres, 13 October 1914

Here 13,000 of the best German soldiers attacked the British and were massacred. For a month, there was desperate hand-to-hand fighting in the woods around the town. As a result of the battle:
- the British suffered 50,000 casualties, with over 8000 deaths, and the BEF was destroyed
- the Germans suffered 20,000 deaths
- the German advance was halted and the Channel ports saved.

Source B: A corporal in the BEF writing home after the First Battle of Ypres

Of the 1100 officers and men that came out to France at the start of the war, we have Major Yeadon and 80 men left. I believe you have plenty of soldiers at home. Well, we could do with a few here.

Tasks

1. Study Source B. What can you learn from Source B about the impact of 1914 on the BEF?

2. Describe what you can see in Source A. What changes do you think would have taken place in Ypres as a result of the battle?

A photograph of British troops in trenches in December 1914

The war in France and Belgium was planned as 'a war of movement'. The rival armies would manoeuvre, trying to outflank their opponents. By Christmas 1914, however, it was clear that neither side was going to achieve a quick victory. The Schlieffen Plan and the German attempt to seize the Channel ports had both failed.

Even so, the Germans showed no sign of giving in and were strong enough to resist any counter-attacks. The war on the Western Front had reached deadlock. No one could deliver the knockout blow. Both sides had lost well over half a million men in the summer and autumn battles. The losses had been so great that there was even talk of a negotiated peace. However, neither side was prepared to accept anything less than complete victory.

The armies of both sides began to dig in where they stood, and soon an elaborate network of trenches was constructed, from the Channel coast to Switzerland (see map on page 37). Trench warfare was supposed to last for the winter and then, in 1915, the war of movement would resume. In fact, the war in the trenches would last for over three years.

Christmas 1914

On Christmas day, at various points along the front, an unofficial truce began and the shooting died away. German soldiers sang carols. British troops responded with their own. They then shouted greetings to each other. Even more surprisingly, in some places men from both sides climbed out of their trenches and walked into **no-man's-land**. There they swapped cigarettes and even played a game of football. Two days later, however, the shooting started again.

Source A: A letter from a British officer to *The Times*, end of December 1914

All this talk of hate, all this fury which has raged since the beginning of the war, was quelled and stayed by the magic of Christmas. Indeed one German in no-man's-land said 'But you are the same religion as us, and today is the Day of Peace!' It is a great hope for future peace when two great nations, hating each other as foes have seldom hated, should on Christmas Day lay down their arms, exchange smokes, and wish each other happiness.

Tasks

1. Study Source A. What can you learn from Source A about the unofficial Christmas Day truce?

2. Imagine you are a British journalist who witnessed the 'truce' of Christmas Day. Write the front page headline and article describing what took place.

3. Using a diagram or illustration, explain the difference between a war of movement and a war of deadlock.

Examination practice

This section provides guidance on how to answer the explanation question using a source and your own knowledge, Question 3, which is worth ten marks.

Question 3 — explanation, using a source and your own knowledge

Use Source C and your own knowledge to explain why the German Schlieffen Plan failed.   (10 marks)

How to answer

- As always, read the question carefully. This is about why the Schlieffen Plan failed. You should know that there were several reasons for this.
- You are going to have to provide at least three reasons, and explain them in detail. Your answer should be about one and a half to two pages long. It should be organised into three or four paragraphs. Every paragraph has to come back to the question.
- You need to start with the source. Follow the numbered boxes to see how to organise your first main paragraph.

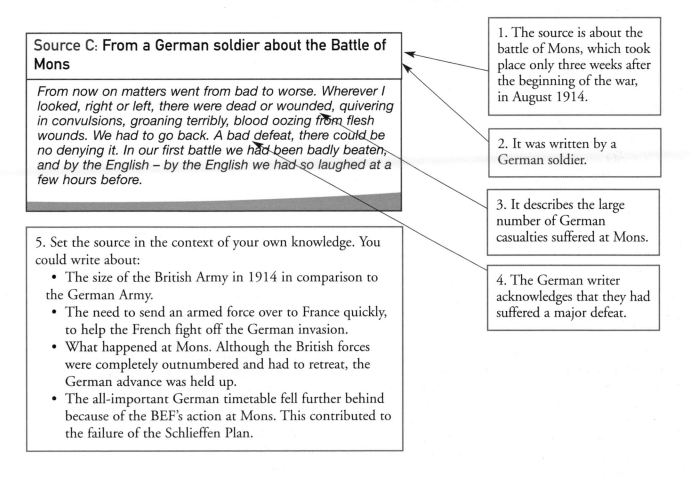

Source C: From a German soldier about the Battle of Mons

From now on matters went from bad to worse. Wherever I looked, right or left, there were dead or wounded, quivering in convulsions, groaning terribly, blood oozing from flesh wounds. We had to go back. A bad defeat, there could be no denying it. In our first battle we had been badly beaten, and by the English – by the English we had so laughed at a few hours before.

1. The source is about the battle of Mons, which took place only three weeks after the beginning of the war, in August 1914.

2. It was written by a German soldier.

3. It describes the large number of German casualties suffered at Mons.

4. The German writer acknowledges that they had suffered a major defeat.

5. Set the source in the context of your own knowledge. You could write about:
- The size of the British Army in 1914 in comparison to the German Army.
- The need to send an armed force over to France quickly, to help the French fight off the German invasion.
- What happened at Mons. Although the British forces were completely outnumbered and had to retreat, the German advance was held up.
- The all-important German timetable fell further behind because of the BEF's action at Mons. This contributed to the failure of the Schlieffen Plan.

STEP 1

A short introduction shows the examiner that you know what you're doing and where you're going.

Say why the German generals designed the Schlieffen Plan and how it was supposed to work.
Say that a number of reasons combined to cause it to fail.

STEP 2

This is the paragraph which we planned on page 30.

Source C shows one reason why the Plan failed.
Use the notes from page 39 to explain why the British action at Mons held up the German advance. German soldiers were exhausted and the Plan was running too late to succeed.

STEP 3

- Explain another reason for the failure of the Plan
- Select good detail from your own knowledge
- Show precisely how the reason you have chosen led to the failure of the Plan

Example:
The Belgian defences were stronger than the Germans expected. They had strong forts at Antwerp, Liège and Namur. The advancing German army had to bring up heavy guns to destroy them. This delay gave time for the French and British to mobilise their armies. The strict timetable of the Schlieffen Plan needed in order to bring Germany a quick victory was running late.

STEP 4

- Explain another reason for the failure of the Plan
- Select good detail from your own knowledge
- Show precisely how the reason you have chosen led to the failure of the Plan

Example:
The battle of the Marne, beginning on 5 September, 1914, marked the failure of the Schlieffen plan. The German army had got to within 65 km of Paris. However, delays caused by the Belgian resistance and the action of the British at Mons meant that the German forces were tired and divided. The French had time to bring up all their available forces. In a battle lasting over a week the German army was forced to fall back. The Schlieffen Plan, to defeat France in 3 to 4 weeks, had failed.

STEP 5

If you have time, write a short conclusion.

The Plan nearly succeeded. Several reasons combined to cause it to fail (if you can think of any more that you have not explained in detail already, just mention them here). The failure of the Plan meant that the war was going to go on for a long time.

5 Britain's contribution to the Western Front 1915–17

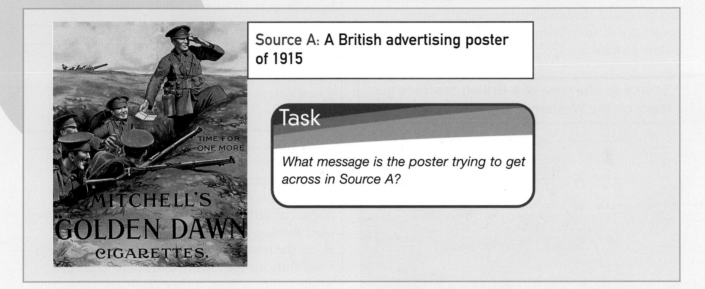

Source A: A British advertising poster of 1915

Task

What message is the poster trying to get across in Source A?

Both sides dug what they believed would be temporary trenches for the winter of 1914–15, fully expecting to break through and resume a war of movement in 1915. However, no such breakthrough was achieved and instead there was deadlock on the Western Front for the next three years. As the trench systems became stronger and more complex, so it became even more difficult to break through. Both sides made major attempts to break the stalemate, most notably the Germans at Verdun in 1916 and the British on the Somme in 1916 and at Passchendaele in 1917. All failed and led to very heavy casualties. However, during the war, there were several attempts to break this stalemate with the introduction of new weapons such as gas, tanks and aeroplanes. Though each of these weapons scored some successes, none was able to give one side a clear advantage and permit a breakthrough. The stalemate continued until 1918.

This chapter answers the following questions:

- What was the nature of trench warfare?
- Why was there a stalemate on the Western Front?
- What part did Haig play in the stalemate?
- Why was there no breakthrough at the Somme?
- How were new methods of warfare used on the Western Front?

Examination skills
In this chapter you will be given the opportunity to answer examples of all the five different types of question on Paper 3.

What was the nature of trench warfare?

Although initially each side dug one line of the trenches, during the course of the next three years the trench systems became stronger and more sophisticated. Eventually there were as many as four lines of trenches with **dug-outs** 10 metres below ground level.

Source A: The crew of a British machine gun team on the Western Front

Tasks

1. *Why was the machine gun in Source A an ideal weapon for defending the trench system?*

2. *Very few soldiers who went over the top were able to reach the enemy trenches. Working in pairs, use the information and diagrams on these two pages to make a list of the obstacles that would have to be overcome in order to reach the enemy lines.*

Dug-outs were the daily living quarters for the troops and their refuge from attack. They could be as deep as 10 metres below ground level.

Each side protected itself with rows of barbed wire, secretly erected or improved at night. These defences were often several metres high and deep.

The trenches were constructed to give the maximum protection to the defenders. The v-shaped walls of zig-zag trenches absorbed the impact of artillery shells and so helped minimise blast damage and injuries to troops further along the trench. The zig-zag shape also made it more difficult for enemy soldiers to capture a whole trench – even if they captured one section they could not fire along the whole length of the trench.

Troops did not often go hungry although there was little variety in their diet. They often ate 'bully' or corned beef, with ten men sharing a loaf of bread.

Cooking facilities were very basic. Some troops had no hot meals for weeks on end. Water was generally brought in petrol cans to the front, where chloride of lime was added to kill the germs. This made it taste awful. In winter the men even melted snow and ice to make tea.

Some soldiers suffered from shell shock, caused by the constant strain of living under shellfire. Early on in the war this mental illness was not understood by the army and many men, unable to fight, were shot as cowards.

Soldiers not only fought but also lived in the trenches. Most days were very monotonous and boring and seemed to pass very slowly. People were killed, but there were few great battles. Men sat around reading or smoking or playing chess. Some wrote letters home.

Diseases were common in the trenches where men crowded together in unhygienic conditions. They all had lice – in their hair, on their bodies and in every part of their clothing. Men were occasionally deloused but the lice would reappear within a few days. There were rats everywhere, feeding on rotting bodies and horse carcasses. They even nibbled the troops as they slept. Much more serious were the epidemics. Germs in food and water led to typhus, cholera and dysentery.

No-man's-land was a desolate area between the two rival trench systems which could be as little as 100 metres wide. Artillery shells had destroyed any drainage ditches, creating a sea of mud and shell craters in which many soldiers drowned.

The soldiers also had to put up with extremes of weather – from snow and frost in the winter to rain on a regular basis. The bottom of the trenches was frequently under at least 30 centimetres of water. Long periods of standing in water led to trench foot where the feet swelled and went completely numb for a few days.

Behind the front line were the reserve trenches in case the front line should be captured. They were also a resting place for the front-line troops. In some places there were even third and fourth lines of trenches. Running between these lines were communication trenches, which were used to move troops and supplies. Everything going up to the front had to use these trenches – fresh troops, water, food, supplies and mail.

There were many dangers:
• Enemy marksmen known as snipers waited for any head that suddenly popped over the parapet. Many unsuspecting new arrivals were killed this way.
• Enemy bombardment, which happened most days, could lead to injury or death from flying splinters and debris.
• Poisonous gas.

Why was there a stalemate on the Western Front?

Both sides made attempts to break through between 1915 and 1917, without success. There were several reasons for the stalemate.

The trench system

In the First World War **infantrymen** were supposed to attack quickly through gaps in the enemy trenches. This proved impossible against trenches that were defended by barbed wire and sandbags. Barbed wire and mud made **cavalry** charges ineffective.

The machine-gun

Machine guns were ideal defensive weapons. They could fire up to 600 rounds a minute and were able to cut down the lines of attackers, causing huge casualties. The German Maxim gun accounted for 90 per cent of Allied victims in the Battle of the Somme (see pages 46–47).

The failure of new weapons

Several new weapons were developed, including the use of poison gas, flame-throwers and tanks (see pages 48–51). None were successful in achieving a breakthrough.

- The invention of the gas mask reduced the effectiveness of poisonous gas.
- The early tanks were low and cumbersome with many breaking down. They were not used properly until 1918.
- Heavy guns could cause considerable damage to enemy trenches but could not destroy the barbed wire or achieve a breakthrough. If anything they slowed down the attacking side, since no-man's land became badly churned up by the bombardment.
- The flame-thrower was unreliable and quite likely to explode and kill the soldier using it.

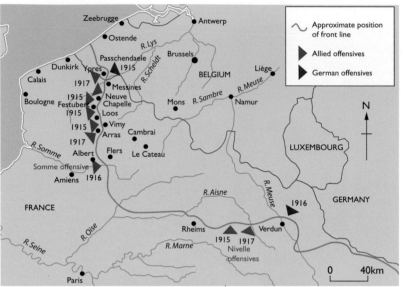

The main offensives on the Western Front, 1915–17

The commanders

Trench warfare was a new kind of fighting. No one really knew how to win a war like this, so the generals fell back on the ideas they had used successfully in past wars, such as mass cavalry or infantry attacks. General Haig even said 'cavalry will have a greater use in future wars'. In fact they were hardly used. The commanders on both sides persisted for three years in the belief that weight of numbers would achieve a breakthrough against machine-guns and barbed wire.

Task

Draw a concept map showing the main reasons for the stalemate and the links between them. Here is an example.

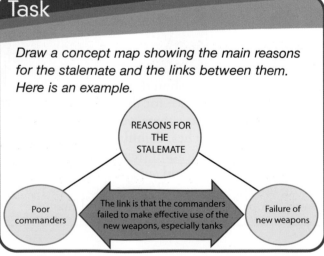

The part played by the British on the Western Front

What part did Haig play in the stalemate?

Sir Douglas Haig was appointed commander of the British forces on the Western Front in December 1915. He has come in for much criticism. He was nicknamed 'The Butcher of the Somme' because of the heavy casualties during the Somme offensive. He was blamed for his failure to break the stalemate.

Evidence for 'The Butcher'

Haig believed in a policy of attrition, which meant wearing the enemy down with constant attacks even if it led to heavy casualties.

Source A: Haig, writing in 1919

In the course of the struggle, losses are bound to be heavy on both sides, for in this the price of victory is paid. There is no way of avoiding this although our total losses in the war may have been greater than were to be expected.

Source B: A letter written to The *Daily Telegraph* in November 1916

We are slowly but surely killing off the best of the male population of these islands. Can we afford to go on paying the same sort of price for the same sort of gain?

Source C: From a school textbook about the First World War, 1985

The High Command, and especially Haig, could not think of any other form of warfare except to throw into battle large numbers of men, month after month. Haig's method of winning the war was clumsy, expensive in loss of life and based on a misreading of the facts.

Evidence against 'The Butcher'

Haig faced a difficult task. Trench warfare was a new kind of fighting.

Source D: Haig, writing in 1919

We attacked whenever possible, because a defensive policy involves the loss of the initiative. The object of all war is victory and a defensive attitude can never bring this about.

Source E: From a book, *Field Marshall Haig*, written by Philip Warner in 1991

If the criterion of a successful general is to win wars, Haig must be judged a success. The cost of the victory was appalling, but Haig's military methods were in line with the ideas of the time, when attrition was the method all sides used to achieve victory.

Source F: From a history textbook, 2001

Haig believed that the key objectives of his offensives were achieved. The Battle of the Somme saved Verdun and the French army. Passchendaele took the pressure off a French army close to breaking point. Some of Germany's best troops were killed in both 1916 and 1917, preparing the way for the Allied successes of 1918.

Tasks

1. Study Source C, D and E. How far do these sources agree about the methods used by Haig? Explain your answer, using the sources.

2. Which of the following statements do you most agree with?
- Haig deserves the title 'The Butcher of the Somme'.
- Haig does not deserve the title 'The Butcher of the Somme'.
Write a paragraph justifying your choice, using evidence from all the sources.

Why was there no breakthrough at the Somme?

In 1916, the British launched a major offensive on the Somme. The battle lasted from July to November and failed to make the expected breakthrough. It cost the British army more than 420,000 casualties, 60,000 of which were on the first day (1 July).

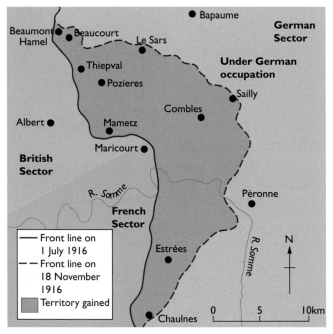

A map showing territory gained by the British in the Battle of the Somme, July–November 1916

The Somme offensive was launched because:
- Haig believed in a policy of attrition, or wearing down the Germans by constantly attacking.
- The British Secretary of State for War, Lord Kitchener, had launched a major recruitment campaign in 1915. As a result, the British army had been strengthened by about one million new recruits. In addition, the British were reinforced by troops from parts of the British Empire, including Australia, New Zealand, Canada, South Africa, India and the Caribbean.
- The Germans had attacked the French fortress system at Verdun in February and the French were desperate for help. They suggested a joint Anglo-French offensive to take the pressure off Verdun.

- The Somme was chosen as it was the area of the front where the British and French armies met. However, it was also the area in which the German defences were strongest.

Source A: Haig, writing after the battle

The German defences consisted of several lines of trenches, well-provided with bomb-proof shelters and protected by wire entanglements forty yards wide, built of iron stakes interlaced with barbed wire. The woods and the villages between the trenches had been turned into veritable fortresses.

1 July 1916

The offensive was preceded by a week-long bombardment, with 1500 guns shelling the German lines continuously. The barrage did not destroy the barbed wire and served only to warn the Germans that an attack was imminent. When the shelling ended, the Germans, who had been sheltering in deep dug-outs, quickly took up their posts at the machine-guns.

The first British soldiers went over the top at 7.30a.m. They had been told to form 'waves' and walk slowly across no-man's land, as there would be no German survivors of the bombardment. In fact they went into the worst slaughter ever suffered by the British army – nearly 20,000 were killed and 40,000 wounded on the first day.

Source B: Sergeant Cook describes it

The first Rifle Brigade advanced in perfect order. Everything was working smoothly. The first line had nearly reached the German front line, when all at once machine-guns opened up all along our front with a murderous fire. We were caught in the open, with no shelter. Men were falling like ninepins.

Source C: A still from *The Battle of the Somme, 1916,* an official film made by the British government to be shown to the public, showing attacks by the British troops

July–November

Despite the losses, Haig, under pressure from the French, continued the offensive. In September tanks were used for the first time (see page 51) but were ineffective. The villages of Beaumont Hamel and Beaucourt were captured using a new tactic, the **creeping barrage** (see page 49), in which the infantry attacked at the same time as the artillery bombarded the German positions. Bad weather finally brought an end to the battle in November.

Source D: An official German photograph of a British soldier killed at the Somme

What did it achieve?

By the time the battle ended, the Germans had been pushed back a little but there had been no breakthrough. By November 1916 the British and imperial forces had lost over 400,000 men.

Source E: Haig's views after the battle

By the third week in November the three main objectives with which we commenced had already been achieved. Verdun had been relieved, the German forces had been held on the Western Front and the enemy's strength had been considerably worn down.

Source F: From an official history of the war

For this disastrous loss of the finest men there was only a small gain of ground to show. Never again was the spirit or the quality of the officers and men so high. The losses were heavy and could not be replaced.

Tasks

1. *How reliable are Sources C and D as evidence of the Battle of the Somme? Explain your answer using Sources C and D and your own knowledge.*

2. *'The Battle of the Somme was a total failure.'*

How far do Sources A–F support this statement? Use details from the sources and your own knowledge to explain your answer.

How were new methods of warfare used on the Western Front?

Once trench warfare had developed and fighting became static, the power of the machine-gun and artillery became evident. New weapons were used during the fighting – for example, gas, tanks, aeroplanes – to try to break the stalemate. When each was introduced it was hoped there would be an immediate breakthrough but this was never the case. This section looks at the use of each of the new weapons.

Gas

Gas was used as early as August 1914, when the French decided to deploy tear gas against the Germans as they advanced through Belgium. The gas was meant to slow the German soldiers but it failed as an active deterrent because it did not kill, nor did it cause panic. The German retaliation came in October when they shelled French positions with a gas that caused violent sneezing attacks. The intention was not to kill the enemy but to render him unable to defend a position, and hence permit a breakthrough. The gas simply failed to harm the enemy.

Source A: An official photograph of British gas casualties, taken in 1918

Source B: From the memoirs of a soldier in the British army, writing about a gas attack in 1916

I was sitting on the fire step, cleaning my rifle, when he [a new recruit] called out to me: 'There's a sort of greenish, yellow cloud rolling along the ground out in front, it's coming ... ' But I didn't wait for him to finish. I grabbed my bayonet, which was detached from the rifle, and I gave the alarm by banging a nearby empty shell case. At the same instant, gongs started ringing down the trench, the signal for Tommy to don his respirator, or smoke helmet, as we call it ... For a minute, pandemonium reigned in our trench – Tommies adjusting their helmets, some running here and there, and men turning out of the dug-outs with fixed bayonets, to man the fire step.

Task

1. *What does Source A tell us about the use of gas in the First World War?*

Types of gas

The first time that an effective poisonous gas was used in the war was at the Second Battle of Ypres in April 1915. Here, chlorine was deployed by the Germans against the French. After this development, each side introduced more devastating chemicals and by 1918 more than 63 different types of poisonous gas had been used. By this time, their use had become widespread, particularly on the Western Front. The German army ended the war as the heaviest user of gas. It has been estimated that the British used 25,000 tons of gas during the war. Deaths from gas after about May 1915 were relatively rare but each side continued to use it because it injured soldiers and also created great inconvenience. Figures show that gas killed about 8000 British soldiers and injured almost 200,000.

Source C: From the poem 'Dulce et Decorum Est' by Wilfred Owen. Owen was a British soldier and poet, killed on 4 November 1918.

Gas! Gas! Quick, boys!
An ecstasy of fumbling,
Fitting the clumsy helmets just in time;
But someone still was yelling out and stumbling,
And floundʼring like a man in fire or lime ...
Dim, through the misty panes and thick green light,
As under a green sea, I saw him drowning.
In all my dreams, before my helpless sight,
He plunges at me, guttering, choking, drowning.

Protection against gas attacks

Gradually, each army developed a means of combating the use of gas. Initially, simple methods were used, and soldiers were even advised that holding a urine-drenched cloth over their face would serve in an emergency to protect against the effects of chlorine. In 1915, British soldiers were given efficient gas masks, but these were not really effective when the Germans began using mustard gas, because this attacked the skin. By 1918 soldiers on both sides were far better prepared to meet the ever-present threat of a gas attack. Filter respirators were standard and proved highly effective.

The creeping barrage

By 1916, both sides had worked out that defending troops could learn to survive artillery bombardment. Deep trenches and bunkers made it much less likely that troops in the target area would be hit. Even after a long barrage, damage inflicted could be relatively quickly repaired to prevent infantry breaking through. This became quite clear on the first day of the Battle of the Somme (see page 46).

As a result, the Allies developed the creeping barrage, which involved artillery fire moving forward in stages just ahead of the advancing infantry. To work, the strategy required precise timing by both the artillery and the infantry and, once started, could not be easily changed. If the soldiers moved too fast they advanced into the shelling and were blown up, and if they were too slow, the enemy had time to recover. The innovation was partially successful – mainly against clearly defined and localised targets. But it was not the breakthrough tactic that the generals had hoped for.

Tasks

2. *Study Sources A, B and C. How far do these sources agree about the effects of gas attacks? Explain your answer, using the sources.*

3. *Source C is a poem. How useful is this source in helping you to understand a gas attack?*

4. *Work in pairs. List reasons to explain why deaths from gas after 1915 'were relatively rare'.*

5. *Why did gas fail to bring the breakthrough that the army leaders had hoped for?*

6. *You are a doctor/nurse on the Western Front. Write a letter home describing your experiences after being involved in helping soldiers after a gas attack.*

Tanks

Source E: From an article in the *Manchester Guardian*, 18 September 1916, describing the tank attack at Flers

You must imagine this huge engine stalking majestically amid the ruins followed by the infantry, drawing the disarmed Germans from their holes in the ground like a magnet … our chaps laughed instead of killing them. Before turning back, the tank silenced a battery of artillery, captured its gunners, and handed them over to the infantry. Finally, the tank retraced its steps to the old British line at the close of a profitable day. The German officers captured in Flers have not yet taken in the scene – the crowded 'High Street' and the cheering bomb-throwers marching behind the travelling fort, which displayed on one armoured side the startling placard, 'Great Hun Defeat. Extra Special!'

Tanks were first used by British forces in September 1916 at the Battle of the Somme but had only limited success. During the next two years they continued to experience mixed fortunes but in the summer of 1918 they did play an important role in the Allied breakthrough of the German lines.

The British wanted a machine that could cross a trench and break through barbed wire. It was specified that any armour plating would have to protect the tank from small arms fire. The first tank was ready for action in early 1916 but it was only by September that there were enough to use in an attack. However, their introduction created tension in the army. The British Commander-in-Chief, Haig, decided to use them, against the wishes of the Commander of the tank corps, who wanted to use tanks only when the army had huge numbers. Haig wanted to use the first 50 immediately because he wanted to be able to boast some success in the Battle of the Somme. As Commander-in-Chief, his decision was final.

The British army used tanks for the first time on 15 September 1916 at Flers during the Battle of the Somme. A total of 49 tanks began the attack but seventeen broke down on the way to the front line and then another nine failed to work when the attack began. Five others became stuck in ditches. Eighteen tanks moved slowly into no-man's-land and were able to capture their objectives. Many Germans ran away, terrified of the new weapon. Over the next three days, gains of over 6 kilometres were made on a narrow front. However, bad weather, shortage of tanks and increased German reinforcements meant that the initial successes could not be built on.

Task

7. How reliable are Sources D and E as evidence of tank attacks in the First World War? Explain your answer using Sources D and E and your own knowledge.

Source F: From *Military Operations: France and Belgium, 1918* by Brigadier-General Sir James E. Edmonds, 1947

The effect of tanks was really only on the morale of the soldiers. Tanks did a good service in crushing machine gun posts and in village fighting. They were less effective in moving across muddy territory where there were huge craters and damaged trenches. From what I saw, it was clear that the infantry liked to see them. Moreover, the enemy constantly exaggerated the numbers that were employed and often reported their presence when there was none. It is evident that the Germans stood in fear of tanks.

Tasks

8. *Work in groups. Each group must produce a case for or against the use of tanks in the First World War.*

9. *How far do Sources D and E support the view of Source F about tank attacks in the war? Explain your answer, using the sources.*

Problems faced by tanks

Slow

Extremely hot inside

Difficult to manoeuvre

Difficult for commanders outside to communicate with the tank crews

Problems faced by tanks

Soon became stuck in the mud

Mechanically unreliable

Machine guns could penetrate the armour

Tanks in the later stages of the war

The first major success of the tank came at the Battle of Cambrai in November 1917, when the entire British Tank Corps of 474 tanks was involved in action against the Germans. The tanks broke through the German lines and the supporting infantry was able to capture 10,000 German prisoners, 123 guns and 281 machine-guns. The success of the tanks was not sustained because there were insufficient infantry reserves to hold the breach.

In the August 1918 offensive (see page 58), 604 tanks assisted an Allied advance of 32 kilometres on the Western Front. Yet, even here, the tanks' problems had not been overcome.

The war in the air

When war broke out in 1914, aeroplanes were still in their infancy. The first flight had only been made in 1903 and military aircraft development was slow because civilian and military leaders did not conceive of aeroplanes as war machines. Source G shows that huge numbers of aircraft were built during the war; however, they did not become a really effective weapon. There were hints at the potential of air warfare towards the end of the war, when aeroplanes were used to support tank attacks at the Battle of Cambrai and also in the 1918 summer offensive (see page 58). The Germans also used them as bombers, bringing terror to parts of south-east England.

Source G: A graph showing aircraft production during the First World War

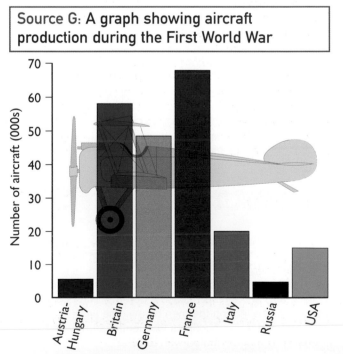

Number of aircraft (000s) vs. Austria-Hungary, Britain, Germany, France, Italy, Russia, USA

The work of aircraft on the Western Front

Aircraft could perform a number of tasks, as the diagram on the right shows. However, they were slow and could not carry large numbers of bombs. At first, pilots had to use pistols or revolvers to defend themselves, but eventually machine-guns were developed, which could fire between the propeller blades. Aircraft were often unreliable and could easily be shot down. For example, in the period March–May 1917, Britain lost 1270. Aircraft were used against soldiers in the trenches, but the aeroplane was not the weapon that brought an end to the stalemate.

Pilots

Almost all the pilots involved in flying aircraft in the First World War were under the age of 25. Many were under 21 and most were sent into combat after about 30 hours of training. The life expectancy of a pilot at the front was quite short.

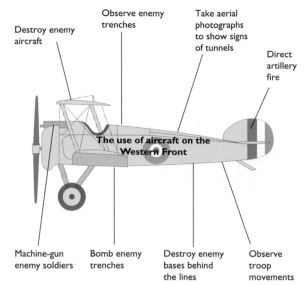

Destroy enemy aircraft

Observe enemy trenches

Take aerial photographs to show signs of tunnels

Direct artillery fire

The use of aircraft on the Western Front

Machine-gun enemy soldiers

Bomb enemy trenches

Destroy enemy bases behind the lines

Observe troop movements

The uses of aircraft during the war

Source H: An artist's impression of British planes attacking German trenches, published in the *Sphere*, a British newspaper, 5 October 1918

The caption in the newspaper read: 'The machines dive on their target pouring out a storm of machine gun bullets, and at intervals release a bomb which falls with tremendous effect on the men below. The work is dangerous and our machines frequently return with their frames and fabrics riddled with bullets.'

Tasks

10. *What can you learn from Source G (page 51) about the use of aircraft in the First World War?*

11. *Look at the diagram that shows the uses of aircraft. Place the uses in order of importance in trying to break the stalemate and explain why you rank them so.*

12. *How useful is Source H as evidence about the use of aeroplanes in the First World War?*

13. *Re-read pages 48–52 and copy out the table below. For each of the weapons, give a mark out of 10 based on its overall effectiveness and usefulness in the war. Then explain how each was effective/useful in the spaces provided.*

	Out of 10	Effective	Useful
Gas			
Tanks			
Aeroplanes			

14. *'New weapons were of little use in the First World War.'*

How far do Sources A (page 48), C (page 49), E (page 50), F (page 51), G (page 51) and H (page 52) support this statement? Use details from the sources and your own knowledge to explain your answer.

Examination practice

On the next two pages there is an example of a complete Paper 3A, containing further examples of all five question types that you will have to answer. The paper will include a separate booklet of the six sources (this page). The five questions are on page 54.

Source A: A photograph of wounded British troops, 1 July 1916

Source B: A British advertising poster of 1915

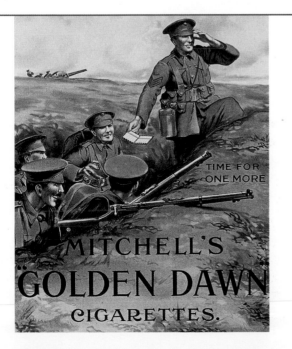

Source C: Sergeant Cook describes the battle on 1 July 1916

The first Rifle Brigade advanced in perfect order. Everything was working smoothly. The first line had nearly reached the German front line, when all at once machine-guns opened up all along our front with a murderous fire. We were caught in the open, with no shelter. Men were falling like ninepins.

Source D: A report from Sir Douglas Haig, British Commander-in-Chief, on the first day of the Somme, July 1916

Yes, we had some casualties. Overall, however, a very successful attack this morning. All went like clockwork. The battle is going well for us and already the Germans are surrendering freely. The enemy is so short of men that he is collecting them from all parts of the line. Our troops are in wonderful spirits and full of confidence.

Source E: From a book, *Field Marshall Haig*, written by Philip Warner in 1991

If the criterion of a successful general is to win wars, Haig must be judged a success. The cost of the victory was appalling, but Haig's military methods were in line with the ideas of the time, when attrition was the method all sides used to achieve victory.

Source F: From the diary of a British soldier, 1 July 1916

It was a bloody disaster. As soon as the signal was given machine-gun fire opened up on us. The heaviest casualties occurred on passing through the gaps in our own wire where the men were mown down in heaps. There were dead and wounded everywhere.

The questions will be in an answer booklet with space below each question for you to write your answer.

Unit 3: Modern World Source Enquiry
Option 3A: War and the transformation of British society, c1903–28

Time: 1 hour 15 minutes

Answer ALL questions.
Look carefully at Sources A to F in the Sources Booklet (page 53) and then answer Questions 1 to 5 which follow.

1. Study Source A.
   What can you learn from Source A about British losses on the first day of the Battle of the Somme?

(6)

2. Study Source B and use your own knowledge.
   What was the purpose of this representation?
   Use details of the painting and your own knowledge to explain your answer.

(8)

3. Study Source C and use your own knowledge.
   Use Source C and your own knowledge to explain why British casualties were so heavy in the battle?

(10)

4. Study Sources D and E and use your own knowledge.
   How reliable are Sources D and E as evidence of Haig's ability as a commander?
   Explain your answer, using Sources D and E and your own knowledge.

(10)

5. Study Sources D, E and F and use your own knowledge.
   Spelling, punctuation and grammar will be assessed in this question.
   Source E suggests that Field Marshall Haig was a successful general.
   How far do you agree with this interpretation? Use your own knowledge, Sources D, E and F and any other sources you find helpful to explain your answer.

(16)

(Total for spelling, punctuation and grammar = 3 marks)
(Total for Question 5 = 19 marks)

The end of the war

ONLY THE NAVY CAN STOP THIS

Source A: A poster published in the *New York Herald,* May 1917. The poster shows a German soldier with a pirate skull-and-crossbones on his helmet and holding a bloody sword as he wades into a tide of women's and children's bodies.

Task

Study Source A and use your own knowledge. Why was this poster published so widely? Use details from the poster and your own knowledge to explain the answer. (Remember how to answer this type of question? For guidance, see page 24.)

Events in 1917 changed the complexion of the First World War. In April the USA entered the war on Britain's side. The **Bolshevik Revolution** in Russia in October resulted in the withdrawal of that country from the war in March 1918. Nevertheless, an end to the fighting was not anticipated. The failure of the German **Spring Offensive** proved to be a turning point. It was followed by the Allied drive to victory and the collapse of Germany in October and early November.

This chapter answers the following questions:

• Why did the Spring Offensive of 1918 fail?
• What part did the British play in the drive to victory?
• How and why did Germany collapse in 1918?

Why did the Spring Offensive of 1918 fail?

In March 1918, Ludendorff, the German commander on the Western Front, decided to launch a series of offensives in a dramatic attempt to win the war.

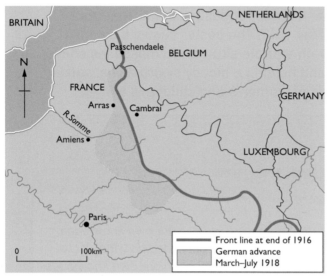

The Western Front and the extent of the German advance by July 1918

Reasons for the offensives

There were several reasons for Ludendorff's decision.

- The USA had entered the war on the side of Britain in April 1917, due to the sinking of US ships by German **U-boats**. Each month, more American troops completed their training, while weapons, ships and aircraft were mass-produced ready for the American entry into Europe. The longer the war went on, the more US troops and supplies would arrive in Europe and the less likely Germany was to win. Ludendorff gambled on winning the war before the Americans could make a decisive contribution.
- The **Bolshevik** takeover in Russia, in October 1917, led to the Russian withdrawal from the war in March 1918. The German army commanders could now transfer about one million troops from the Eastern to the Western Front. For a time, the Germans would outnumber the Allied troops.
- The Allied armies on the Western Front had been weakened by the events of 1917. In May 1917 there had been a series of **mutinies** in the French army, which had greatly reduced the morale of the French troops. Moreover, the British had suffered heavy losses during the Third Battle of Ypres from July to November 1917.
- The British naval blockade of Germany was beginning to cause serious shortages and hunger among the civilian population.
- Germany's allies, Turkey and Austria, were both in trouble and were talking of surrender.

The German attacks

Ludendorff decided to target the British defences, believing they were still exhausted by the events of 1917. Moreover, he was convinced that if the British were driven back, this would lead to the surrender of the French armies. His aim was to cut through the Somme and then wheel north-west to cut the British lines of communication. Ludendorff knew that an ordinary frontal assault would fail against machine-guns. Instead he used lightly equipped German 'storm troops', trained to attack not in waves but in small groups, avoiding British strong points and probing until they found a weak spot where they could push right through.

The German attack, code-named Operation Michael, began on 21 March 1918, using artillery and mustard gas. German troops advanced in small groups through the swirling mists. In many places visibility was less than 10 metres and the British troops were quickly overpowered. The Germans advanced 8 kilometres on the first day as the British soldiers retreated in chaos.

Despite the early confusion, the British forces were not destroyed. A new defence line was hastily formed and troops were rushed from Italy and the Middle East to reinforce the British defences. Haig did not panic but on 23 March issued his famous 'Backs to the Walls' orders (see Source B).

The Allies now decided to place all their armies on the Western Front under one commander, the French General Foch. He was able to co-ordinate the Allied defences against the German attacks. In April the Germans attacked again in the Ypres area, hoping to break through and capture the Channel ports. Again they had early success but the British were not defeated and built new defences. Finally, in May, Ludendorff launched attacks on the French defences near Verdun. The French retreated over 60 kilometres and the Germans were within sight of Paris. Many Parisians packed their belongings and fled the capital. However, resolute French defence, with the help of newly arrived American troops, withstood the German advance.

The situation in July 1918

Ludendorff's gamble had failed and the offensive drew to a close at the end of July. It failed because:

- The Germans had moved too quickly. The supporting forces, bringing essential supplies of munitions and food as well as fresh troops, could not keep up with the advance. Advancing German soldiers had also wasted valuable time looting French shops in the areas they captured.
- The Germans had suffered appalling casualties – 880,000 by the end of July.
- There was no breakthrough and the Germans had a much greater area to defend with a makeshift, hastily assembled trench system. Paris, Ypres, Arras, Amiens and Verdun were still controlled by the Allies.
- The German troops were exhausted and low in morale. They had been told that the Allies were hungry and unhappy. Yet, when they captured Allied trenches they found plentiful supplies.

Tasks

1. Study Source A. What can you learn from Source A about the German attacks of March 1918?

2. Study Source B and use your own knowledge. What was the purpose of this order? Use details from the order and your own knowledge to explain your answer.

3. Make a list of reasons why the German gamble failed. Place these in a mind map in rank order, from the most important at 12 o'clock, clockwise, to the least important.

What part did the British play in the drive to victory?

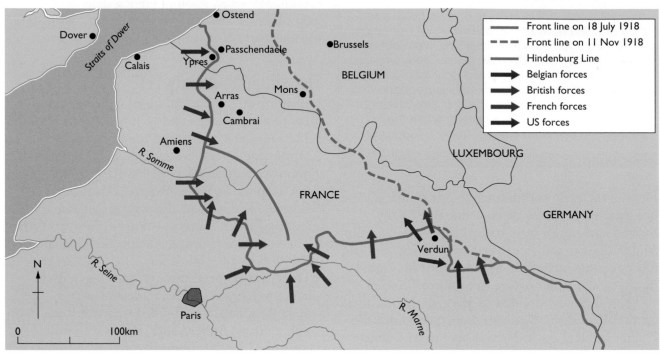

The Allies' summer and autumn offensives, 1918

The failure of Operation Michael was the sign to the German High Command that they could not win the war. The Allied counter-attack began on 8 August 1918 and eventually led to the defeat of Germany.

The two sides

The Allies had several advantages over the Germans, as the box below shows.

German weaknesses	Allied strengths
• The German soldiers were exhausted after the offensives of March–July 1918. Ludendorff said he needed 200,000 fresh troops each month to continue the war. However, he was told that the reserves could only provide 300,000 for the whole of the next twelve months. Moreover, the Germans had a much larger area to defend with fewer troops and hastily set-up defences. • The German war effort had been seriously disrupted by the effects of the British blockade (see page 60). There was a shortage of chemicals as well as iron ore, which meant the Germans had to reduce production of poisonous gas and weapons.	• The Allies were being constantly reinforced by the arrival of fresh American troops. This greatly increased the morale of the British and French soldiers. • The unified command structure under General Foch enabled the Allies to co-ordinate their attacks on the German defences. • Haig provided effective leadership, enabling the advancing British armies to make maximum use of air cover, gas and tanks. • The Allies used the tanks to great effect to spearhead attacks and force gaps in the German trenches, which could be exploited by advancing infantry troops.

The part played by the British on the Western Front

The Allied attacks

On 8 August the Allies hit back against the Germans. There was an artillery bombardment and then an aerial attack, which was followed by infantry and 456 tanks. Canadians, Australians, Belgians, French and British troops combined to burst through the German defences and force the Germans back. At Amiens, the British captured 30,000 Germans and 400 field guns. Ludendorff later described 8 August as the 'black day of the German army'.

The Germans gave up land they had won following Operation Michael and were then forced to retreat beyond the Hindenburg Line, the defensive system they had created in 1917. It was extremely well fortified with **pillboxes** and concrete dug-outs. On the day of the counter-attack, the German army began to retreat on a 320-kilometre front with 27,000 soldiers killed and 15,000 prisoners.

By the end of September, Germany's allies were crumbling. Austria-Hungary was exhausted and Turkey was seeking an **armistice**. On 28 September, Bulgaria surrendered and within the next five days Austria-Hungary and Turkey signed armistices.

By late October, the coast of Belgium had been liberated. In a single day the Allies advanced 13 kilometres from Ypres, which was more than they had managed in months of bitter fighting the years before.

Source A: Ludendorff, writing in later years

The 8 August was the blackest day of the German army in the history of the War. This was the worst experience I had to go through. Our losses reached such proportions that the Supreme Command was faced with the necessity of having to disband a series of divisions.

Source B: An official British photograph showing some of the German troops captured at Amiens in August, 1918

Source C: General Rawlinson, the commander of the British Fourth Army, described the Battle of Amiens in his diary

The surprise on the 8 August was complete. The Germans had no idea that the Canadians were at my front, and believed them to be at Kemmel. The tanks were all up to time, and did splendidly, and some of our armoured cars got right through the German lines and surprised the headquarters of a German corps at breakfast. We have practically eaten up seven Prussian divisions. I am very proud to have commanded so magnificent an army in this historic battle.

Tasks

1. Study Source B and use your own knowledge. Why was this photograph published so widely? Use details from the photograph and your own knowledge to answer the question.

2. Study Source C. What can you learn from Source C about the events of 8 August 1918?

3. Study Sources A and B. How reliable are Sources A and B as evidence of the events of August 1918? Explain your answer using Sources A and B and your own knowledge.

4. Working in pairs, devise a series of headlines for British newspapers on 9 August 1918.

How and why did Germany collapse in 1918?

On 11 November 1918, the Germans agreed to an armistice. The surrender of Germany was partly due to the military defeat on the Western Front but also due to developments in Germany.

The effects of the British blockade

The British navy blockaded German ports from early 1915, and the effects on the German people were soon apparent. By the end of the second year of the war, imports had fallen to almost half of 1913 levels, and agriculture was severely hit by the inability to import fertilisers. With most of Germany's ships trapped in her own ports, iron ore could no longer be imported from Sweden. This meant that Germany had to rely on seizing materials from the countries it had conquered.

By the winter of 1917, the supply of potatoes had run out and the only real alternative was turnips. This is why the winter of 1917–18 is known as the 'Turnip Winter'. The outbreak of influenza in October 1917 added to the growing discontent inside Germany. The civilians held on, but the constant queuing for food was eroding enthusiasm for the war.

Source B: A member of the German government speaking to a colleague in October 1918

We have no meat. Potatoes cannot be delivered because we are short of trucks. We need 4000 trucks a day. Fat is unobtainable. The shortage is so great it is a mystery to me what the people of Berlin live on.

Source A: A queue for potatoes in Berlin, late 1917

The part played by the British on the Western Front

At the beginning of 1918, there was rationing in Germany and the average food intake was 1000 calories. The death rate was 37 per cent higher in 1918 than it had been in 1913. Moreover, further outbreaks of influenza weakened many civilians and soldiers in the spring and summer of 1918.

The Kiel mutiny

At the end of October, German sailors at Kiel mutinied and refused to accept the order to put to sea. The German admirals planned to attack the British navy in a desperate bid to break out of the British blockade but there was little support from the sailors for the plan. The army was not sent to crush this mutiny because the government could not be confident that the soldiers would not join the sailors in their revolt. Workers and soldiers took over Kiel and nearby ports. Cities throughout Germany joined the revolt.

The Armistice

On 9 November Kaiser Wilhelm II abdicated and fled to the Netherlands. On the following day a German republic was set up under Friedrich Ebert, leader of the Social Democratic Party. On 11 November the new government concluded an armistice with the Allies. The Germans had to:
• withdraw from the rest of Belgium and France
• surrender all weapons and release prisoners of war
• surrender all warships and U-boats
• allow Allied troops into Germany.

Tasks

1. *How reliable are Sources A and B as evidence of the problems caused by the British blockade? Explain your answer using Sources A and B and your own knowledge.*

2. *Devise a caption for Source C that could have been used by the sailors who mutinied.*

3. *Explain why the British blockade was important in bringing about the defeat of Germany.*

Source C: A photograph taken at the German port of Wilhelmshaven on 1 November 1918. It shows sailors who have taken control of the warship and have unloaded ammunition.

Key Topic 3: The Home Front and social change

Source A: A First World War army recruiting poster

TO THE YOUNG WOMEN OF LONDON

Is your 'Best Boy' wearing Khaki? If not don't YOU THINK he should be?

If he does not think that you and your country are worth fighting for – do you think he is WORTHY of you?

Don't pity the girl who is alone – her young man is probably a soldier – fighting for her and her country and for YOU.

If your young man neglects his duty to his King and Country, the time may come when he will NEGLECT YOU.

JOIN THE ARMY TODAY!

Task

Study Source A. What can you learn from Source A about recruiting methods during the First World War?

This key topic examines the impact of the First World War on the people of Britain. The war was the first one to affect the whole population and changed the relationship of the government with its people. By the end of the conflict, the government had introduced laws ranging from conscripting men into the armed forces to limiting the hours when pubs could open. Britain would never be the same again. The topic also analyses the crucial part played by women in the war and how it led to further changes in society.

Each chapter explains a key issue and examines important lines of enquiry as outlined below:

DORA, censorship and propaganda

Source A: A postcard issued by the British government during the First World War. Britannia (left) is about to smack the Kaiser's hand.

Task

Study Source A and use your own knowledge. Why was this source published so widely in Britain?

Unlike the many other wars that Britain had fought in, the First World War was one that involved the whole population. Most families were unable to escape the loss of a loved one and entire communities lost large numbers of young men. Moreover, as the war went on, the government found that it had to interfere more and more in the everyday life of its citizens. The government introduced restrictions on work and leisure and, in 1916, finally introduced **conscription**. Without government interference, Britain could not have engaged in the war for so many years.

This chapter answers the following questions:

- What was the Defence of the Realm Act?
- Why did the government introduce censorship?
- Why was propaganda important in the war?

Examination skills
In this chapter you will be given guidance on how to answer the question analysing the reliability of a source, Question 4, which is worth ten marks.

What was the Defence of the Realm Act?

What was the Defence of the Realm Act?

When the war began in August 1914, the government wanted to ensure that the whole population would support the war effort. In addition, it sought to defend Britain from any internal threats. In order to carry out these aims, the government passed the Defence of the Realm Act (DORA) on 8 August. DORA meant that the government had broad emergency powers and anyone who did not comply with any new wartime regulations could be heavily fined or imprisoned.

Several Liberal MPs were against DORA, because it infringed basic freedoms. The first person to be arrested under DORA was John Maclean, a Communist, for making statements that demanded an end to the war. He was fined £5 but refused to pay and was then imprisoned for five nights.

> **Source A: Part of a London police notice restricting the use of lights under DORA**
>
> **POLICE NOTICE**
> AS TO LIGHTS IN LONDON
>
> The Secretary of State for the Home Department, under the powers conferred on him by Regulation 11 of the Defence of the Realm (Consolidation) Regulations, 1914, has made an order which contains the undermentioned provisions: –
> In all brightly lighted streets and squares and on bridges a portion of the lights must be extinguished so as to break up all conspicuous groups or rows of lights: and the lights which are not so extinguished must be lowered or made invisible from above by shading them or by painting over the tops and upper portions of the globes: provided that while thick fog prevails the normal lighting of the streets may be resumed.
> Sky signs, illuminated fascias, illuminated lettering and lights of all descriptions used for outside advertising or for the illumination of shop fronts must be extinguished.

The key features of the Defence of the Realm Act

- The government could imprison people without trial.
- The government could requisition buildings and land which it considered necessary for the successful conduct of the war.
- The military could take over any piece of land without the agreement of the owner.
- The government could censor newspapers.
- The government introduced British Summer Time to give more daylight working hours.
- The sale of drugs and alcohol was strictly controlled. Alcoholic beverages were watered down and pub opening times were restricted to noon–3p.m. and 6.30p.m.–9.30p.m. Customers were not allowed to buy a round of drinks. Before the war, pubs had opened between 5.30a.m. and half past midnight.
- Shops had to close at 8p.m.
- Lights had to be put out or kept to a minimum at night.
- Flagpoles or any other equipment that could be used for signalling were banned.
- People needed a permit to keep homing pigeons.
- It was illegal to:
  - photograph military bases or to try to get information from military personnel
  - talk about naval or military matters in public places
  - own or use equipment relating to phones or telegraphs without a government permit
  - light a bonfire
  - fly a kite
  - feed bread to wild animals
  - buy binoculars.

Why did the government introduce censorship?

The government introduced postal and press **censorship** to prevent any contact with the enemy and to ensure that the war was always presented to the public in a positive light. Despite complaints about infringements on personal liberty, the government could point to censorship being successful. Postal censorship showed that there were 34,500 British citizens with alleged ties to the enemy. There were 38,000 people who were placed under suspicion 'by reason of any act or hostile association' and a further 5246 who were associated with **pacifism** and **anti-militarism**.

Source B: From *The Pity of War* by N. Ferguson

Wartime Britain became, by stages, a kind of police state. In 1916 the Press Bureau, assisted by the secret service department, scrutinised over 38,000 newspaper articles, 25,000 photographs and about 300,000 telegrams. As The Nation magazine put it – 'it was a domestic tragedy of war that the country which went out to defend liberty is losing its liberties one by one and that the government that began by relying on public opinion as a great help has now come to fear and curtail it'.

The Defence of the Realm Act meant that the national press was subject to censorship and the amount of information reaching the press from the front was always limited. The *Daily Mail*'s reporting was so subjective that the troops created their own alternative paper, sarcastically called 'The *Daily Liar*'. The *Globe* newspaper was prevented from publishing for two weeks in 1915 after it wrote a story about a senior politician, but most newspapers exercised self-censorship

throughout the war. A good example of this was the sinking of the battleship HMS *Audacious* on 27 October 1914. This was not reported until the end of the war. Some restrictions were rather silly: for example, weather reports were not to be printed in newspapers, on the grounds that they were useful to the enemy.

Tasks

1. *Copy the table below. Choose the four most important and the four least important points from the Defence of the Realm Act and explain your choices.*

Most important	Least important

2. *Study Source A. What can you learn from Source A about DORA?*

3. *Study Source B. What is meant by the term 'police state'?*

4. *Write a paragraph attacking the government's decision to ban the publication of The* Globe *newspaper.*

5. *Working in pairs, prepare a defence of censorship to present to the class.*

Why was propaganda important in the war?

Propaganda was a way in which the government could influence the general public in regard to important issues such as recruitment and conscription, the economy and success at the front, and morale in general. To control propaganda, the government set up the War Propaganda Bureau in September 1914. Within a year, it had published over 2.5 million books, speeches, pamphlets, photographs and war paintings.

The problem for the War Propaganda Bureau was the maintenance of morale. Despite press censorship, casualty lists were published in the newspapers and the general public was aware that large numbers of soldiers were being killed. Clearly, propaganda had to put across a message that the war was just and was worth fighting. Most importantly, it had to demonise the enemy.

The Bureau had well-known writers such as Thomas Hardy and H.G. Wells working for it. One of the first pamphlets to be published was *Report on Alleged German Outrages* (1915). The purpose of the pamphlet was to show the public that the Germans had tortured Belgian civilians. Two other famous pamphlets were *To Arms!* by Sir Arthur Conan Doyle and *The New Army* by Rudyard Kipling.

The War Propaganda Bureau also commissioned films, which were shown all over the country. If there was no cinema in a town, then the film would be projected from a lorry onto any available large wall. The film *Battle of the Somme* showed real and simulated scenes from the Somme campaign. For once, it showed images of dead soldiers. Many of the scenes were shot near Southampton. The film was extremely popular and was seen by more people than any other film during the war.

The Ministry of Information was created in 1918 and was headed by Lord Beaverbrook, the owner of the *Daily Express* newspaper. He ensured that other senior figures in the newspaper industry were given posts within the ministry in order to oversee propaganda policies. Lloyd George was then accused of controlling the most important people in the press.

Source B: A drawing of the execution of Edith Cavell, 12 October 1915. Edith Cavell was a British nurse who worked for the Red Cross in Belgium. She was tried as a spy and executed by a German firing squad for helping British soldiers to escape to the Netherlands. This drawing was published widely in Britain.

MISS EDITH CAVELL
MURDERED
October 12th 1915
REMEMBER!

Source D: An illustration showing a charge by soldiers of the Liverpool and Scottish regiments to recapture a trench taken by the Germans, who had taken it using flame throwers

Source C: A British government poster, published in 1918, to persuade people to buy war savings certificates

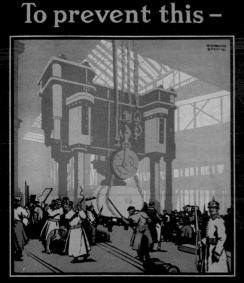

To prevent this –

BUY
WAR SAVINGS CERTIFICATES
NOW

Tasks

1. *Study Source A. What message is the cartoonist trying to put over?*

2. *Devise a caption for Source A.*

3. *Why was it important for the War Propaganda Bureau to have authors such as Conan Doyle working for it?*

4. *How reliable are Sources B and C as evidence of British attitudes towards Germany in the First World War? Explain your answer using Sources B and C and your own knowledge.*

5. *Why was there concern about members of the press working for the Ministry of Information? Explain your answer.*

6. *Study Source D and use your own knowledge. Why was this illustration published so widely in newspapers in Britain during July 1916? Use details from the illustration and your own knowledge to explain your answer.*

Examination practice

This section provides guidance on how to answer the reliability question, Question 4, on Paper 3, which is worth ten marks.

In answering the reliability question, you must analyse various aspects of two sources. To reach the top level, you need to cover both fully. The content and the nature, origin and purpose (NOP) of a source should be considered and out of this will emerge an evaluation of the source's reliability.

In order to gain higher-level marks for this question you have to use **both** what you know about the **content** of the source (the topic) and its **NOP** to judge its reliability. The NOP is found in the provenance of the source – the information given above or below it. A good tip is to highlight or underline key words in the provenance that show the reliability of the source. An example of this approach is given in Source A on page 69.

There is also guidance in the box below about what to consider for the NOP of a source.

NOP means:

N Nature of the source.
What type of source is it? A speech, a photograph, a cartoon, a letter, an extract from a diary? How will the nature of the source affect the reliability of its evidence? For example, a private letter often provides very reliable evidence because the person who wrote it generally gives their honest views.

O Origin of the source.
Who wrote or produced the source? Are their views worth knowing? Are they giving a one-sided view? When was it produced? It could be an eyewitness account. What are the advantages and disadvantages of eyewitness accounts?

P Purpose of the source.
For what reason was the source produced? For example, the purpose of adverts is to make you buy a product. How will this affect the reliability of the source?

Question 4 – reliability

How reliable is Source A as evidence of the German attack on Scarborough in the First World War? Explain your answer.

How to answer

Although in the exam you will be asked to compare two sources, in the question above we look at one source to help you build your skills in analysing a source. Best answers have two angles: the content of the source (what it tells you) and its NOP.

First let us concentrate on content. You should think about the following questions:
1. From what you know, does the source seem accurate?
• What does it mention? How does this compare to your own knowledge about the event? This is known as your contextual knowledge and helps you decide the reliability of the source.

For example:

> Source A gives the view that the Germans killed women and innocent children, and the view that Germans had killed civilians was common. Civilians were killed in other places on the east coast. It shows that Germans were barbaric and this is what many people felt at the time.

2. Are there any limitations to the content?
• Does it give a very limited or inaccurate view?
• What does it not tell us about the event or person?

For example:

> Source A has limited reliability because it does not give all the figures of those killed in Scarborough and implies only women and children were killed. In fact the shelling killed more people in Hartlepool, where 86 died.

Now let's move on to NOP. This page uses NOP to test Source A as evidence of the German attack on Scarborough in 1914. Notice that it is reliable in some ways and unreliable in others. You should try to write something on both sides.

Unreliability

Nature It is of limited reliability because it is a poster. This means it has to provide an immediate impact with a direct meaning. If it had been so bad why was a photograph not used?

Source A: A government poster, which was published after the German shelling of Scarborough in 1914

Reliability

Nature It is partly reliable because it is a poster that gives an image of what happened.

Origin It is reliable because it was published directly after the attack and has some statistics.

Origin It was a government poster and the government would always want to make the enemy look awful. It would be typical of government propaganda.

Purpose It is reliable as an example of government propaganda that tries to play on the fear of Germany and the barbarity of the Germans. It shows a little girl and a baby outside the building, which is meant to make people feel angry. Its appeal to men would probably make them join the army.

Purpose It is unreliable because it has given an exaggerated number of those killed. It implies that large numbers were killed in Scarborough, which is untrue. Notice that the content of the source seems unreliable – you wouldn't rely on its accuracy. It is, however, very reliable evidence of British government propaganda (see opposite). So the same source can be reliable **and** unreliable. It depends what you want to know.

Now have a go yourself

Answer Question 4 on page 68 using all the guidance given on these two pages. Make a copy of the planning grid below and use it to plan your answer. Include the value and limitations/unreliability of the source. If you need further guidance on this, look back to page 68.

Planning grid			
	Reliability	**Limitations and unreliability**	**Own knowledge of this item**
Contents			
What does the source tell you?			
NOP			
Nature			
Origin			
Purpose			

The reliability of two sources

For Paper 3 you need to evaluate the reliability of two sources.

Question 4 – reliability

How reliable are Sources B and C as evidence of propaganda in Britain during the First World War? Explain your answer using Sources B and C and your own knowledge.

Source B: A still from *The Battle of the Somme*, 1916, an official film made by the British government to be shown to the public, showing attacks by the British troops

Source C: *The Battle of the Somme*, written in 1917 by the official British War Correspondent Philip Gibb

At 7.30a.m. on 1st July the British infantry left their trenches and attacked but they could not check our men or stop their progress. After the first week of battle the German General Staff had learnt the truth about the qualities of those British New Armies which had been mocked and caricatured in German comic papers. The Germans learnt that these 'amateur soldiers' had the qualities of the finest troops in the world – not only extreme valour but skill and cunning, not only a great power of endurance under the heaviest fire, but a spirit of attack which was terrible in its effect. The British were great bayonet fighters. Once having gained a bit of earth or a ruined village nothing would budge them unless they could be blasted out by gunfire.

How to answer

- Explain the reliability and limitations of the contents of the first source. Add here information from your own knowledge about this topic.
- Explain the reliability and unreliability of the first source, using its NOP.
- Explain the reliability and limitations of the contents of the second source. Add here information from your own knowledge about this topic.
- Explain the reliability and unreliability of the second source, using its NOP.
- In your conclusion give a final judgement on the relative reliability of each source. Say which is more reliable and explain why you have reached that judgement.

Make a copy of the grid on page 69 to plan your answer for each source.

Below is a writing frame to help you:

Source B is reliable because (contents) it suggests ....

Moreover Source B is also reliable because of (NOP)..

However, Source B has limitations because (contents) ....

Furthermore, Source B is also unreliable because (NOP) ....

Source C is reliable because (contents) it suggests ....

Moreover Source C is also reliable because of (NOP)..

However, Source C has limitations because (contents)..

In addition, Source C is unreliable because (NOP)..

In conclusion Source B/C is more reliable then Source C/B because it..

Recruitment and rationing

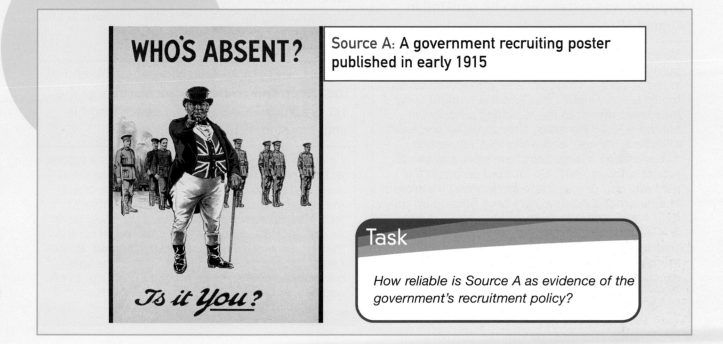

WHO'S ABSENT?

Is it You?

Source A: **A government recruiting poster published in early 1915**

Task

How reliable is Source A as evidence of the government's recruitment policy?

The surge to join the army in Britain in August 1914 was matched by a similar surge among the rest of the combatants in Europe. War had been expected for some years and the Germans had been cast as the villains for some time. Yet, within only a few months, the number of recruits fell alarmingly and various schemes were used to persuade men to enlist. Eventually, the government was forced to introduce conscription. Another measure that the government introduced, after months of trying to avoid it, was food rationing. These two measures were a sharp indication of how much the government had been pushed into interfering in the lives of ordinary British citizens.

This chapter answers the following questions:

• Why did recruitment to the armed forces change during the war?
• What were the key features of conscription?
• Why was conscientious objection such an issue?
• Why was rationing introduced and what were its key features?

Examination skills

In this chapter you will be given further guidance on how to answer the question analysing the reliability of a source, Question 4, which is worth ten marks.

Why did recruitment to the armed forces change during the war?

Source A: From *With a machine gun to Cambrai* by George Coppard, written in 1968. Coppard was sixteen when he enlisted in August 1914.

News placards screamed out at every street corner, and military bands blared out their music in the streets of Croydon. This was too much for me to resist. I knew I had to enlist straight away. I presented myself to the recruiting sergeant at Mitcham Road Barracks, Croydon. The sergeant asked me my age, and when told, he replied, 'Clear off son. Come back tomorrow and see if you're nineteen, eh?' So I turned up again the next day and gave my age as nineteen. I attested in a batch of a dozen others and, holding up my right hand, swore to fight for King and Country. The sergeant winked as he gave me the King's shilling, plus one shilling and nine pence ration money for that day.

When the war broke out on 4 August 1914, there was a tremendous rush to join the British army. On 6 August, Parliament agreed an increase in army strength of 500,000 men. Shortly after this, Lord Kitchener, Minister for War, issued his first call to arms. This was for 100,000 volunteers, aged between 19 and 30, at least 1.6 metres tall and with an expanded chest size greater than 86 centimetres. The common phrase was that the war would be 'over by Christmas' and that it would be quite a 'lark'. Across the nation, men of all ages joined up and many young boys lied about their age so that they could enlist (see Source A). There were not enough guns and uniforms for the recruits and, when training began, some had to use sweeping brushes as stand-ins for rifles.

As the number of recruits increased, it was possible to form units that became known as Pals Battalions. In Accrington, a Pals Battalion led to a full strength unit (1000 men) being formed by mid-September. The battalion comprised brothers, cousins, friends, workmates and neighbours. Similar battalions were formed across the north of England – in cities such as Leeds, Sheffield and Liverpool. The East Yorkshire Regiment had four battalions of Hull Pals with nicknames like The Commercials, The Sportsmen, The Tradesmen and T'others.

Source B: From an interview, after the end of the war, with Private George Morgan, of the 1st Bradford Pals Battalion, describing his enlistment in 1914

I thought it would be the end of the world if I didn't pass the medical. People were being failed for all sorts of reasons. When I came to have my chest measured (I was only sixteen and rather small) I took a deep breath and puffed out my chest as far as I could and the doctor said 'You've just scraped through.' It was marvellous being accepted. When I went back home and told my mother she said I was a fool and she'd give me a good hiding; but I told her, 'I'm a man now, you can't hit a man.'

A terrible postscript to this recruitment was the first day of the Battle of the Somme when thousands of the Pals were killed. The Accrington Pals Battalion suffered appalling losses. Of the 720 who participated, 584 were killed, wounded or missing in the attack and the Leeds Pals lost about 750 of the 900 men in the battalion.

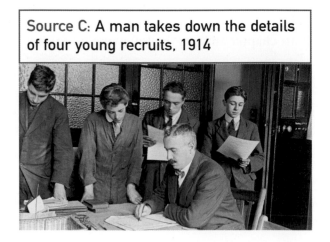

Source C: A man takes down the details of four young recruits, 1914

The Home Front and social change

Source D: Number of recruits to the British army August 1914–December 1915. Lord Kitchener, Minister for War, set a target of 150,000 recruits per month during this period.

August 1914	298,923
September 1914	462,901
October 1914	136,811
November 1914	169,862
December 1914	117,860
January 1915	156,290
February 1915	87,896
March 1915	113,907
April 1915	119,087
May 1915	135,263
June 1915	114,679
July 1915	95,413
August 1915	95,980
September 1915	71,617
October 1915	113,285
November 1915	121,793
December 1915	55,152

Source: From Statistics of the Military Effort of the British Empire during the Great War *(HMSO)*

Source E: From the memoirs of a First World War soldier

The most effective recruiting agents, however, were the women and girls who handed out white feathers to the men not in uniform and not wearing a war service badge.

However, the pace of volunteering slowed in late 1914 and by the end of 1915 the number of recruits did not meet the required total. The government was unwilling to introduce conscription and tried to stimulate recruitment by introducing the National Registration Act in July 1915. All men between the ages of 15 and 65 who were not already in the military had to register. The results showed that there were almost five million men of military age who were not in the forces, of whom 1.6 million were in **protected jobs**.

In October 1915, the government introduced the **Derby Scheme**, which encouraged men to enlist voluntarily, or 'attest' to an obligation to enlist if they were asked. It was agreed that single men would be called up before married men. Men who 'attested' under the Derby Scheme were given an armband with a red crown as a sign that they had volunteered. By early 1916, only 38 per cent of single workers and 54 per cent of married workers had 'attested'.

Tasks

1. Study Source A. What can you learn from Source A about recruiting in August 1914?

2. As a class, work out the average height and chest size of all boys in the group. Compare the average with the average demanded by Kitchener for 19–30-year-olds in 1914.

3. What were the Pals Battalions? Research whether there were Pals Battalions in your area and find out what happened to them at the Battle of the Somme in July 1916. The local history section in your town library should have some material.

4. How reliable are Sources B and C as evidence of recruiting in 1914? Explain your answer using Sources B and C and your own knowledge.

5. What does Source D tell you about recruitment in the years 1914–15?

6. What was the Derby Scheme?

7. Study Source E. What was meant by the term 'white feather'?

What were the key features of conscription?

The continuing lack of recruits pushed the government into introducing conscription. It did so in two phases. First in January 1916, The Military Service Act was passed.

The act conscripted all men who:
- on 15 August 1915 were resident in Great Britain
- who had attained the age of 19 but were not yet 41
- on 2 November 1915 were unmarried or a widower without any dependent children.

The government was still concerned at possible shortages of manpower and, in May 1916, amended the Military Service Act of January.

The act conscripted all men who:
- had been at any time resident in Great Britain since 4 August 1914
- had attained the age of 18 but were not yet 41.

The government also gained the right to re-examine men previously declared medically unfit for service.

There was some opposition to conscription and 50 Liberal and Labour MPs voted against the first act. Many **trade unions** opposed it because they thought the government might extend conscription to industrial work as well as military service. **Conscientious objectors** also opposed the measure.

Tasks

1. *Suggest reasons why the Derby Scheme and partial conscription were not successful.*

2. *Study Source A and use your own knowledge. Why was this poster published so widely across Britain?*

Daddy, what did YOU do in the Great War ?

Source A: A British government recruiting poster, published in 1915

Why was conscientious objection such an issue?

Once conscription was introduced in 1916, the government was faced with the problem of those men who refused to serve in the armed forces. Groups such as 'The Stop the War Committee' had opposed the war from its outbreak and the 'No Conscription Fellowship' had been formed to fight compulsory military service.

Those who challenged the idea of conscription were called conscientious objectors. Some, like the **Quakers**, rejected the call-up on religious grounds, some rejected it on political grounds and others said they were pacifists. There were some who made claims based on disability, that their work was of national importance, or they ran a business.

If they rejected their **call-up papers**, they could attend a tribunal, which would assess their case. Some of the conscientious objectors (sarcastically called 'conchies' or 'cuthberts') offered to carry out civilian war work provided they were not under military law (they were called 'alternativists'). Others volunteered for work in the army provided that it did not involve the use of weapons. About 7000 pacifists agreed to perform non-combat service in the army. This usually involved working as stretcher-bearers at the front line, an occupation that had a very high casualty rate.

However, there were those conscientious objectors who wanted nothing to do with the war. These were the 'absolutists'. There were about 1500 'absolutists' and they refused to be swayed from their beliefs. They were imprisoned and experienced terrible conditions; 71 died in jail and 31 went mad.

Source A: **Conscientious objectors doing hard labour, breaking rocks in prison during the First World War**

Source B: A cartoon published in the *Daily Mirror*, 1917

Source C: From a No Conscription Fellowship pamphlet, 1916

Fellow citizens:
Conscription is now law in this country of free traditions. Our hard-won liberties have been violated. Conscription means the desecration of principles that we have long held dear; it involves the subordination of civil liberties to military dictation; it imperils the freedom of individual conscience. We re-affirm our determined resistance to all that is established by the Act. We cannot assist in warfare. War, which to us is wrong.

Source D: From an account of the treatment of a conscientious objector whose tribunal appeal failed and was then handed over to the army in 1916

The breaking process was begun on Gray (the conscientious objector) by the bombing officer who used his powers of persuasion by means of tapping his ankles to bring him to attention. Subsequently he threw a live grenade at Gray … After successive days of worsening treatment, Gray was stripped naked, a rope tightly fastened around his abdomen and he was then pushed forcibly and entirely immersed in a filthy pond in the camp grounds eight or nine times in succession and dragged out each time by the rope. The pond contained sewage. Gray eventually gave in and obeyed army orders after his will was broken.

Source E: Part of an account of the treatment of Howard Marten, a conscientious objector, when he was imprisoned after his appeal to the tribunal failed

We were placed in handcuffs and locked in the cells and tied up for two hours in the afternoon. We were tied up by the wrists to horizontal ropes about five feet off the ground with our arms outstretched and our feet tied together. Then we were confined to cells for three days on 'punishment diet' – four biscuits a day and water … Rats were frequent visitors to the cells. There were twelve prisoners in a cell which measured 12 feet square.

Source F: These Red Cross volunteers were Quakers and were opposed to fighting on religious grounds. Unless they volunteered for medical support roles, they could be imprisoned.

Tasks

1. *Study Source A. What can you learn from Source A about conscientious objectors?*

2. *Study Source B and use your own knowledge. What was the purpose of this cartoon? Use details of the cartoon and your own knowledge to explain your answer.*

3. *Construct a mind map to show the reasons why men refused to accept conscription.*

4. *Study Source C. What can you learn from Source C about the views of the No Conscription Fellowship?*

5. *Study Sources D, E, and F. How far do these sources support the view that the treatment of conscientious objectors was unfair? Explain your answer, using the sources.*

Why was rationing introduced and what were its key features?

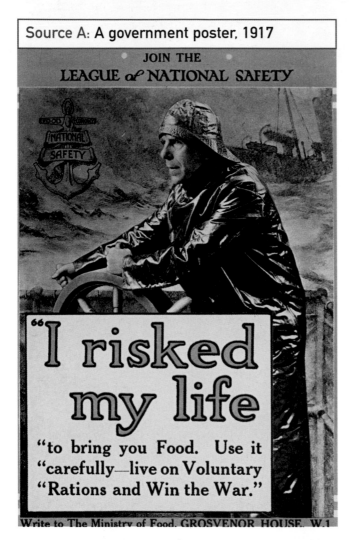

Source A: A government poster, 1917

tonnage). The huge loss of ships in April meant that Britain had only six weeks' supply of wheat left and very little sugar. However, the U-boat threat was overcome by the introduction of convoys. Merchant ships would travel in large numbers under the protection of naval destroyers. Destroyers used **depth charges** to attack U-boats and this new weapon did fend them off. Although U-boats continued to sink ships, the losses were gradually reduced, and the threat of starvation that Britain faced in mid-1917 receded. Convoys protected 24,604 vessels in 1917 and only 147 were sunk.

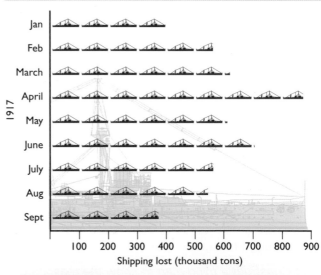

Source B: A graph showing losses of Allied ships in 1917

Shipping lost (thousand tons)

As Britain's population had grown in the nineteenth century, it became necessary to import food to make good the shortfall in British domestic production. When the war started, most of Britain's imported food came from the USA and Canada.

The Germans tried to **blockade** British ports but dared not risk its navy and as a result came to rely on its U-boats (submarines). In February 1917, the Germans decided to attack any merchant ship in the North Atlantic that might be taking food to Britain.

In April 1917, German U-boats sank 866,000 tons of merchant vessels (a quarter of Britain's total

Tasks

1. *Study Source A. What message is the poster trying to put across?*

2. *What does Source B tell us about losses of Allied ships in 1917?*

3. *Explain how the U-boat threat was overcome.*

Food shortages

As a result of shortages, food prices had risen quite sharply in 1916 and they continued to do so in 1917. Despite the 1917 grain harvest being the best on record in Britain, queues for food were a common sight and people began to resent this.

The government encouraged people to eat less bread but this was not realistic because for most it was a cheap and filling food. Meat and other alternatives had become too expensive and potatoes were often in short supply. The King and Queen led the voluntary scheme to cut down food consumption but there was great resentment among the poorer people who saw that those with money could buy food, whatever the cost.

Towards the end of 1917, there was a period of panic buying, and food shortages once again forced the government to act. The Ministry of Food introduced the rationing of certain food items. Ration cards were issued and everyone had to register with a butcher and grocer. As with most other areas of government control, many people accepted it, even though they did not like the idea. Rationing food was intended to guarantee supplies for all people, not to reduce consumption, and it solved the problems of rising prices and food queues.

Item rationed	When rationing began	When rationing ended
Sugar	31 December 1917	November 1920
Butter	May 1918	May 1920
Margarine	May 1918	February 1919
Lard	May 1918	December 1918
Meat	May 1918	December 1919
Jam	May 1918	April 1919
Tea		This was not rationed nationally but its distribution was controlled by national registration of customers, based on 2 oz (50 grams) per person, from July to December 1918

Source C: A government poster, 1917

SAVE THE WHEAT AND HELP THE FLEET

EAT LESS BREAD

Tasks

4. *Explain why rationing was introduced.*

5. *Study Source C and use your own knowledge. What was the purpose of this poster? Use details of the poster and your own knowledge to explain your answer.*

Examination practice

This section provides further guidance on how to answer the reliability question, Question 4 on Paper 3, which is worth ten marks. For guidance on how to answer this question well, see page 68–70.

Question 4 – reliability

How reliable are Sources A and B as evidence of the treatment of conscientious objectors? Explain your answer using Sources A and B and your own knowledge.

How to answer

You are being asked whether you can trust what each source is suggesting each, and then compare them.

- Compare what the source suggests with your own contextual knowledge. Does it seem truthful? If so, then that is part of the way to saying that is reliable. If not, or there are bits of the history missing, then that is part of the way to saying it is unreliable.
- Examine the nature, origin and purpose (NOP) of the source with reference to reliability.

A reminder of what to consider for NOP is on pages 68–69. Below is an example of how to approach this for Source A. Have a go yourself for Source B.

Nature
It is part of an article intended for a specific audience. This means it is less reliable because it was written to encourage people to support the conscientious objectors.

Origins
It is reliable because it is by a conscientious objector who is giving details of punishments at that time.

Purpose
It is less reliable because it is trying to make people sympathise with conscientious objectors and it lacks support.

Contextual knowledge
It is reliable because we know there was harsh treatment of conscientious objectors, and that some died or went mad.

Cross-referencing
It is reliable because both say the treatment of conscientious objectors was harsh, but Source A emphasises this more.

> **Source A: From a June 1917 letter by James Brightmore, a conscientious objector, published in the *Manchester Guardian*, which was sympathetic towards conscientious objectors**
>
> *I was bullied horribly when I was tried and sentenced to 28 days' solitary confinement. I was confined in a pit which started at the surface at three feet by two and tapered off to two feet six inches by 15 inches. The bottom is full of water and I have to stand all day long on two strips of wood just above the water line. There is no room to walk about and sitting is impossible. Already I am half mad.*

> **Source B: From a 1922 book about conscientious objectors by John Graham, a Quaker**
>
> *The conscientious objector seemed to most people to be merely a shirker. The women he knew cut his acquaintance. His mother and his brothers often jeered at him at home. He was chosen by his employer to be dispensed with, and so left open to be punished for his refusal to serve without the business exemption [some men could be excused military service if they did important jobs such as mining] he might otherwise have had. Shirker, coward, dog were the words they were thought to deserve.*

The part played by women

Source A: A women munitions workers' football team from the AEC Munitions Factory at Beckton, London

Task

Study Source A and use your own knowledge. Why was this photograph publicised? Use details from the photograph and your own knowledge to explain the answer.

With the outbreak of war in August 1914, the three women's suffrage societies, the **WFL**, the **NUWSS** and the **WSPU** (see page 7), all decided to suspend their campaign for the vote and support the war effort. The massive recruitment for the armed forces resulted in a shortage of workers, especially in heavy industry, and the employment of women in traditional men's jobs. The contribution of women to the war effort did change attitudes and led to the Representation of the People's Bill, which gave votes to women over the age of 30 in 1918.

This chapter answers the following questions:

• Why were women needed in the war effort?
• What contribution did women make to the war effort?
• What was the impact of women's role in the war?

Why were women needed in the war effort?

The outbreak of the war brought a truce between the suffragettes and the government. Emmeline Pankhurst (see page 8) organised meetings and processions to publicise the part women could play and rallied women behind the war effort. In return, all existing prison sentences were pardoned.

> **Source A:** The newspaper *Suffragette* appeared on 16 April 1915 displaying the slogan below
>
> **IT IS A THOUSAND TIMES MORE THE DUTY OF THE MILITANT SUFFRAGETTES TO FIGHT THE KAISER FOR THE SAKE OF LIBERTY THAN IT WAS TO FIGHT ANTI-SUFFRAGE GOVERNMENTS.**

Mrs Fawcett, the leader of the NUWSS (see page 6), called a similar truce and offered to serve the country.

> **Source B:** From a letter written by Mrs Fawcett to members of the NUWSS in August 1914
>
> *Now is the time for effort and self-sacrifice by every one of us to help our country. Let us show ourselves worthy of citizenship, whether our claim to it be recognised or not.*

Indeed the **suffragists** worked to persuade the men of Britain to join the army. Other women's organisations tried to boost recruitment. The Order of the White Feather encouraged women to give white feathers to young men who were not in the armed forces. The white feather was the symbol of a coward. The Mothers' Union published posters urging mothers to encourage their sons to join up.

As more men volunteered to join the armed forces in the years 1914 to 1916, they had to be replaced in the factories and on the farms. However, it was events in 1915 that encouraged an increase in employment of women. In April it became clear that there were serious shortages of shells and bullets for the British armed forces on the Western Front, causing the 'shell scandal'.

David Lloyd George was appointed Minister of Munitions. He was a keen supporter of employing women in the munitions industry and worked closely with Emmeline Pankhurst to organise a march publicising the recruitment of women. This was the first time the government had accepted that women could play a vital role in winning the war. The government drew up a register of women who were available for work. Later in 1915 the government set up its own munitions factories, which recruited mainly female workers.

Many male employers refused to employ women. The turning point came when conscription was introduced in 1916 (see page 74). At this point many factory owners finally realised they needed to take on women to replace the male workers who had joined the army.

> ## Tasks
>
> 1. *Study Source A. What can you learn from Source A about the attitude of the suffragettes after the outbreak of the First World War?*
>
> 2. *Study Source B. Why was this letter sent to members of the NUWSS? Use details from the letter and your own knowledge to explain the answer.*

What contribution did women make to the war effort?

Before the First World War there were few employment opportunities for women except in nursing, unskilled factory work and **domestic service**. Moreover, female workers were paid far less than their male counterparts for doing similar (or the same) jobs. The war brought about the employment of women in a far greater range of jobs, in both industry and agriculture, which were generally much better paid.

Munitions work

About 60 per cent of all workers employed in making shells were women and by 1918 247,000 women were employed in government munitions factories. Munitions work was tiring and dangerous. As the war went on, shifts got longer and longer. By 1917 they were working 12-hour shifts, seven days a week, packing explosives and **cordite** charges into bullets and shells.

Source A An official photograph of women workers packing fuse heads in the Coventry Ordnance Works during the First World War

In August 1916, medical reports publicised the effects on women of handling TNT explosives. These included breathing difficulties, digestion problems, blood poisoning and even brain damage.

The chemicals also caused their hair to fall out and turned their skin yellow. This earned them the nickname of the 'canaries'.

Source B: **From the diary of a Voluntary Aid Detachment (VAD) cook at a munitions factory, 22 July 1917**

Today I was shown over the factory as a great favour. First I saw cordite made into charges. Then I was shown the lyddite works. This is a bright canary yellow powder (picric acid). NS comes to the factory in wooden tubs. It is then sifted. The house, (windows, doors, floor and walls) is bright yellow, and so are the faces and hands of all the workers. As soon as you go in the powder in the air makes you sneeze and splutter.

Munitions work was also very dangerous and some people were killed when munitions factories blew up. In 1917 a fire in the Silvertown Munitions Works in East London caused an explosion that killed 69 people and injured 400. Nevertheless, most women in munitions factories were better paid than in their previous work. They were looked after by women welfare supervisors, and there were separate toilets in factories, nutritious food in the canteens and government-provided nurseries.

Tasks

1. *Working in pairs, devise two further entries for the diary in Source B, describing the conditions in munitions factories.*

2. *How reliable are Sources A and B as evidence of female employment in munitions factories during the First World War? Explain your answer using Sources A and B and your own knowledge.*

Heavy industry and transport

By the end of the war, almost 800,000 women had taken up work in engineering industries. The evidence soon showed that even with little training they were as skilled as men. The war made it acceptable for women to work in shipyards and brickyards, as plumbers, signalwomen and even electricians. Some of them worked as highly skilled lathe-operators and carpenters. Others worked in breweries, tanneries, linoleum factories, caustic soda works and for window-cleaning firms.

Moreover, during the war, the male dominated trade unions were very suspicious of women coming into factories and doing men's jobs. They were worried that this would bring down wages and that men would lose their jobs for good. However, the government reached agreement with the unions. Women were to be paid the same as men but would only have the men's jobs 'for the duration of the War'.

In addition women were employed in public transport as tram and bus drivers and conductors. There was even a Women's Voluntary Police Service in most of the major cities.

Source C: A government poster of 1917

The Women's Land Army

There was also a shortage of workers on the land, as many farm workers had joined the army. Women were asked to sign up for the Women's Land Army and did work that would have been done mainly by men before the war and were paid the same wages. The work was often hard – stone-picking, weeding, pulling turnips, ploughing, milking and haymaking. Nearly 18,000 women worked on farms full-time and 30,000 part-time.

Women's armed forces

Women also went to the front line, working as nurses and driving ambulances. Most of the women who went to the front belonged to some sort of organisation. Women in the First Aid Yeomanry (FANYs) and the Voluntary Aid Detachment (VADs) helped nurses and men in the Royal Army Medical Corps. By September 1916, there were over 8000 VADs working in military hospitals. The women were not paid for the work they did.

In 1917 the government set up the women's armed forces to carry out non-fighting duties such as office work, driving, cleaning and cooking. First came the Women's Army Auxiliary Corps (WAAC), organised like the army with uniforms and officers. This was soon followed by the Women's Royal Air Force (WRAF) and the Women's Royal Naval Service (WRNS).

Source E: **A member of the WAAC describes her living conditions in a camp in France**

We eventually arrived at Etaples. Our camp was composed of long wooden huts. I was allocated a bed along with about 19 other girls. The beds were composed of hard mattresses and a pillow and two rough blankets. Each morning before going to work we had to fold the blankets and place them with a pillow at the bottom of the bed. It wasn't very comfortable sleeping without sheets.

Tasks

1. *Study Source C and use your own knowledge. What was the purpose of this poster? Use details from the poster and your own knowledge to explain the answer.*

2. *How reliable are Sources C and D as evidence of the work done by women during the First World War? Explain your answers using Sources C and D and your own knowledge.*

3. *Study Source E. What can you learn from Source E about the WAAC?*

4. *Write a brief article for a national newspaper in 1917 about women in uniform. Your article should include:*
   - *a catchy headline*
   - *an explanation of the different women's organisations*
   - *your views on this change.*

What was the impact of women's role in the war?

The First World War did bring some changes in the position of women (especially the vote), although in other respects, particularly employment, attitudes remained much the same.

Social change

The war resulted in much greater freedom for some women. With fewer men around, chaperones for wealthier girls became less common. Full wage-packets and better pay meant that women had money to spend. Some went to the cinema or on bicycle trips, or went shopping in town unsupervised. Women drank in pubs and smoked in public. Older people were scandalised, whilst troops returning from France were amazed, especially when they saw women in uniform, some even wearing trousers for the first time.

Source A: From an article in the *Daily Mail*, September 1915

The wartime business girl is to be seen at night dining out in restaurants in London. Before she would never have had her evening meal in town unless in the company of a man friend. But now, with money and without men, she is dining out more and more. The meal of course is accompanied by the customary cigarette.

Source B: From a letter, published in the *Glasgow Herald*, 1916

To observe how men speak and write about women today is vastly amusing to us. We have not changed with the war. It is only that in some instances the scales have fallen from the men's eyes. In the hour of Britain's need her sons have realised that if victory was to be won they could not afford to hem women in with the old restrictions.

Female employment

The war seemed to improve employment opportunities for women, who were able to prove that they could do many of the jobs previously only done by men and sometimes do them better.

Source C: From a report carried out by the National Employers' Federation in 1918

Quality
Sheet metal – Women's work better than men's output.
Aircraft woodwork – Women equal to men in most areas.
Cartridge production – Women equal to men.
Shell production – Women's work poorer than men's.
Quantity
Sheet metal – Women's production equal to 99 per cent of men's output.
Aircraft woodwork – Women's production equal to men's.
Cartridge production – Women's production equal to men's. In some cases 20 per cent more.
Shell production – Women's production behind that of men.

However, there was much opposition during the war to the employment of women, especially from male employers, workers and trade unions, who questioned their ability to do the job.

Source D: From a report sent to the Home Secretary by the president of the transport union, February 1917

I would point out to you that already a very serious dispute has taken place at Croydon a few months back when two women were being taught to drive tramcars resulting in a cessation from work for many weeks, also upon women being appointed as mail drivers the men ceased work immediately, and as a result the women have since been withdrawn.

Moreover, once the war ended, women were expected to give up their wartime jobs and return to their pre-war employment.

Source E: From an article in the *Southampton Times*, 1919

Women still have not brought themselves to realise that factory work, with the money paid for it during the War, will not be possible again. Women who left domestic service to enter the factory are now required to return to the pots and pans.

Source F: A table showing the changes in female employment, 1914–1920

	1914	1918	1920
Domestic service	1,500,000	1,100,000	900,000
Transport	250,000	450,000	425,000
Government and teaching	210,000	900,000	310,000
Agriculture	90,000	500,000	510,000
Office	20,000	100,000	80,000

The vote

The First World War did result in certain women getting the vote. This was partly due to the contribution many women had made to the war effort, which did much to convince politicians such as Lloyd George and Asquith that women had earned the right to vote. In 1918, Parliament finally passed the Representation of the People Act. This gave the vote to all men of 21 years of age or over and to most women aged 30 or over. Moreover, women were allowed to stand for Parliament and become MPs (see Chapter 10, pages 93–96).

Tasks

1. *How reliable are Sources A and B as evidence of changes in position of women during the First World War? Explain your answer using Sources A and B and your own knowledge.*

2. *Study Sources C, D and E. How far do Sources C, D and E agree about the impact of the war on female employment? Explain your answer, using the sources.*

3. *Study Source F. What can you learn from Source F about female employment in the years 1914–20?*

4. *Make a copy of the following pair of scales.*

- *On the left-hand side, give evidence of progress for women in the years 1914–18.*
- *On the right-hand side, give evidence of lack of progress. Which side of your scales has greater evidence?*

5. *'The First World War brought great progress in the position of women.'*

How far do Sources A–F support this statement? Use details from the sources and your own knowledge to explain your answer.

Key Topic 4: Economic and social change

Source A: A miner, Tom Hughes, describes conditions underground in the 1920s

You crawl down to whatever position you are on the coal-face, usually about 120 yards, dragging your tools with you. You need to crawl because it is two feet high. If anybody has an accident everybody helps. For example, one man got crushed – we were not too far in then, only two miles. There were six of them carrying him out and I was at the side holding his tongue. I had to do this because he kept swallowing it. We had to walk because we were not allowed to ride on the wooden wagons.

Task

Study Source A. What can you learn from Source A about working conditions for miners in the 1920s?

This key topic examines the changing role of women in the years after the First World War, especially the extension of the vote and changes in employment and their social position. It explains the long-term causes of the General Strike of 1926, including the industrial **militancy** of the years before and after the First World War, Black and Red Friday and the Samuel Commission of 1926. The last chapter examines the reasons for the failure of the General Strike, looking at government organisation and preparations and the mistakes of the **Trades Union Congress (TUC)**. It ends by explaining the effects of the strike on the **trade union** movement and the coal industry.

Each chapter explains a key issue and examines important lines of enquiry as outlined below:

Chapter 10 The changing role of women 1918–28 (pages 89–96)
- What changes were there in women's work after the war?
- In what ways did the social position of women change?
- What were the reasons for and the importance of the extension of the franchise?

Chapter 11 Industrial unrest 1918–27 (pages 97–107)
- What effects did the years 1914–21 have on trade unions?

- Why were there problems in the coal industry after 1918?
- What were the causes, events and results of Black and Red Friday?
- Why was the Samuel Commission important?

Chapter 12 The General Strike of 1926 (pages 108–116)
- What happened during the General Strike?
- How prepared and organised was the government?
- Why did the TUC call off the General Strike?
- Why did the General Strike fail?
- What were the effects of the General Strike?

10 The changing role of women 1918–28

FREE AND INDEPENDENT.

THE THREE LEADERS (*together*). "WANT A PILOT, MADAM?"
NEW VOTER. "NO, THANKS."

Source A: A cartoon published in a British magazine, after the 1928 Representation of the People Act was passed. The three political party leaders are Ramsay MacDonald (Labour), Stanley Baldwin (Conservative) and Lloyd George (Liberal).

Task

What does Source A tell us about the position of women in 1928?

The position of women in Britain did change in the first years of the twentieth century. The First World War had a tremendous impact on how women were perceived, and some historians have said that they became more 'visible'. It is evident that legislation, especially granting the vote, did give some equality, but many of the gains made in the war were soon lost in peacetime. For many women, life in 1928 differed little from life at the beginning of the century.

This chapter answers the following questions:

• What changes were there in women's work after the war?
• In what ways did the social position of women change?
• What were the reasons for and the importance of the extension of the franchise?

What changes were there in women's work after the war?

Source A: From a letter to *The Times* from Sir George Barnes MP, 1920

There are still a good many young women who are now at work only for 'pin-money'. They should be replaced by the ex-soldier in all cases where he could do the work. If I were an employer just now, I would have every enquiry made about my women workers. I would weed out all those not dependent on their own work for means of living.

In 1919, the government passed the Restoration of Pre-war Practices Act which meant that women working in the civil service, who had taken men's jobs, now had to give them up. Women working in the munitions industry were given two weeks' pay and a return ticket home, and female civil servants were dismissed. By 1920, more than one million women who had found employment in the war were no longer employed.

The employment situation differed across the country. Many women in the south-east were able to find employment in the 'new' industries, such as making domestic appliances and radios. However, there were fewer opportunities in the north, in the 'old' declining industries such as coal mining and ship building.

A married woman was still expected to give up work and, by 1928, about 90 per cent of married women remained at home to look after the children. Everywhere, the message was that motherhood and employment were incompatible. By 1928, the most common employment for women was still in domestic service, just as it had been in 1903. Despite the progress made in the First World War, employment, pay and opportunities for women had scarcely changed by 1931 (see table on page 91).

The Great War was a temporary victory for women. If there had been a major change in society then women would not have been asked to take on greater responsibilities in the Second World War because they would have already been employed in a very broad range of jobs.

Yet there were some positive changes. In 1919, Parliament passed the Sex Disqualification Act, which made it illegal to exclude women from jobs because of their sex. Women could now become solicitors, barristers and magistrates. The first female **Justice of the Peace** was appointed on 31 December 1919 and the first female solicitor qualified three years later.

Source B: From a book written in 1992 about the women's movement in Britain in the twentieth century

The declining profitability of the textile industry was one which hit women's employment significantly. The feminists' reservation was that women were rushing into jobs at a very young age, without trying to take advantage of education and training, and were consequently perpetuating their status as low-level, low-paid, temporary workers.

Source C: From a book about women in the First World War, written by a feminist historian in 1981

There are many familiar features of women's work in the 1920s. They were low-paid, confined to few trades, encouraged to leave work on marriage, and excluded by unions or employers from trades classed as skilled; even when their work was quite complex it was not seen as being skilled.

Source D: A table showing women in work and their earnings, 1911–31

Year	Single women	Married women	All women	Average female earnings
1911	70%	10%	35%	44% of men's
1931	71%	10%	34%	48% of men's

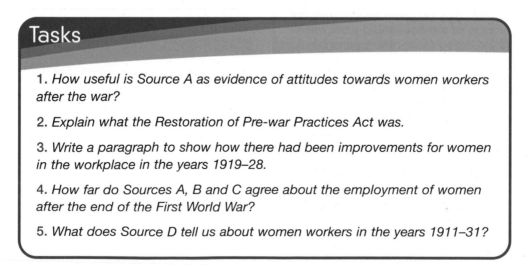

Women at work in a British paper factory, 1925

Tasks

1. *How useful is Source A as evidence of attitudes towards women workers after the war?*

2. *Explain what the Restoration of Pre-war Practices Act was.*

3. *Write a paragraph to show how there had been improvements for women in the workplace in the years 1919–28.*

4. *How far do Sources A, B and C agree about the employment of women after the end of the First World War?*

5. *What does Source D tell us about women workers in the years 1911–31?*

1. *How reliable are Sources A and B on page 93 as evidence about giving women the vote? Explain your answer using Sources A and B and your own knowledge.*

2. *What can you learn from Source C (on page 93) about giving women the vote?*

Importance of the extension of the franchise

Source D: **A photograph of women queuing up to cast their votes for the first time in a general election, 14 December 1918. This was published widely across Britain.**

In early 1918, the Representation of the People Act was passed and this enfranchised some 8.4 million women. The act also allowed women to stand for Parliament and become MPs.

The act enfranchised women who met one of the following criteria:
- over 30 years of age and a **householder**
- over 30 years of age and the wife of a householder
- over 30 years of age and an occupier of property with an annual rent of £5 or more
- over 30 years of age and a graduate of a British university (no property qualification was needed).

The act enfranchised men who were over 21 years of age, or over 19 years of age if they had fought in the war.

Criticisms of the act

Many women who had worked at the front, in the fields and in munitions factories were under 30 and therefore did not get the right to vote.

A total of 22 per cent of women 30 years of age and above were excluded from the right to vote because they were not property owners or did not rent property at a rate of £5 per year or more. These women were invariably working class.

Many women saw the act as a failure because it still classed them below men.

Some males were still able to vote in more than one constituency (where they lived, owned property or a business or were linked to a university).

Source E: Gwendolen Guinness, Conservative MP for Southend-on-Sea, commenting on the 1918 act in 1928

As regards the last extension to the franchise in 1918, it was granted to a large extent in consequence of the part women had taken in the great national effort during the War. But, as a matter of fact, that Act was so adjusted to exclude those women who had done most in industry to make up the great shortage of labour.

Source F: Asquith's comments about the women electors in the Paisley by-election, 1920

There are about 15,000 women on the electoral roll – a dim, impenetrable, for the most part unreachable element – of whom all that one knows is that they are for the most part hopelessly ignorant of politics, credulous to the last degree, and flickering with gusts of sentiment like a candle in the wind.

Women had their first opportunity to vote in the general election in December 1918.

Several of the women involved in the **suffrage** campaign stood for Parliament. Only one, Constance Markiewicz, standing for **Sinn Fein**, was elected. However, as a member of Sinn Fein, she objected to the British government's policies in Ireland and she refused to take her seat in the House of Commons. In 1919, Nancy Astor was the first woman in England to become an MP and take up her seat when she won a by-election in Plymouth. Margaret Bondfield, a Labour MP, became parliamentary secretary to the Minister of Labour in 1924 and was the first female to have a seat in the Cabinet. She became the first cabinet minister in 1929 on being appointed Minister of Labour.

Source G: Women in British parliamentary elections 1918–29

Year	Women candidates	As % of candidates	Total MPs	Women MPs	Women as % of MPs
1918	17	1	707	1	0.1
1922	33	2.3	615	2	0.3
1923	34	2.4	615	8	1.3
1924	41	2.9	615	4	0.7
1929	69	4.0	615	14	2.3

Tasks

3. *Study Source D and use your own knowledge. What was the purpose of publishing this photograph? Use details of the photograph and your own knowledge to explain your answer.*

4. *Prepare a brief speech criticising the 1918 Representation of the People Act.*

5. *How reliable are Sources E and F as evidence of attitudes towards giving women the vote? Explain your answer using Sources E and F and your own knowledge.*

6. *What does Source G tell us about the involvement of women in politics in the 1920s?*

The changing role of women 1918–28

95

1928 Equal Franchise Act

By 1924, it was clear that the extension of the franchise had been successful and many politicians thought it reasonable to amend the 1918 act. A bill was introduced in March 1928 to give women the vote on the same terms as men. There was little opposition in Parliament to the bill and the Equal Franchise Act became law on 2 July 1928. As a result, all women over the age of 21 could now vote in elections. Some sarcastically called it the 'flapper vote'.

It was estimated that, as a result of the act, the electorate comprised around 12,250,000 men and about 14,500,000 women.

Source H: A cartoon from the magazine *Punch*

THE JUDGMENT OF GLADYS.

Tasks

7. *Study Source H and use your own knowledge. What was the purpose of the cartoon? Use details from the cartoon and your own knowledge to explain your answer.*

8. *Study Source I. What did Wilkinson mean when she said a woman needed 'furniture' in order to vote?*

9. *Re-read the sections on women in this book (pages 89–96). Copy and complete the table below.*

Evidence of progress for women 1903–1928	Evidence against progress for women 1903–1928

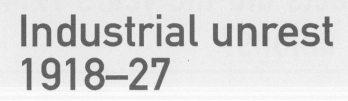

11 Industrial unrest 1918–27

Source A: A cartoon from 1921 about the Triple Industrial Alliance. The three heads represent the three trade unions – the railways, transport and miners.

Task

Study Source A. Why was this cartoon published so widely? Use details from the cartoon and your own knowledge to explain your answer.

In May 1926 there was a general strike in Britain. This was the culmination of industrial militancy in the years before and after the First World War and problems in the coal industry. Indeed, a general strike almost occurred in 1921, on what became known as Black Friday, but the trade unions backed down; and, four years later, on Red Friday, when the government intervened. The report of the Samuel Commission in March 1926 set off a chain of events that led to the start of the General Strike that year.

This chapter answers the following questions:

• What effects did the years 1914–21 have on trade unions?
• Why were there problems in the coal industry after 1918?
• What were the causes, events and results of Black Friday and Red Friday?
• Why was the Samuel Commission important?

Examination skills
In this chapter you will be given guidance on how to answer the question analysing an interpretation, Question 5, which is worth sixteen marks.

What effects did the years 1914–21 have on trade unions?

The trade union movement grew bigger and stronger in the years before, during and after the First World War.

Industrial militancy, 1910–14

In the years before the First World War there were a series of official and unofficial strikes that challenged the Liberal government. This was partly due to the influence of **syndicalism**, a movement originating in France. Syndicalists believed workers had the right to control industries they worked in. Their ultimate weapon was 'direct action' or strikes, culminating in a general strike.

The British trade union movement came closer to realising this idea of a general strike with the formation of the Triple Industrial Alliance in 1913. The three largest unions agreed on the idea of **sympathetic** strike action. If one member came out on strike the other two would come out in sympathy. This would effectively lead to a general strike, as the country would be paralysed, thus giving the unions more bargaining power. The three unions were:

- **Miners Federation of Great Britain and Ireland (MFGB)**. In 1910, 30,000 miners in South Wales went on strike for higher wages. Two years later, the **MFGB** organised the Miners' Minimum Wage Strike. Instead they were given district minimum wages.
- **National Union of Railwaymen (NUR)**. Railway workers had come out on strike in 1911 for improved wages. Two years later, the various railway unions amalgamated to form the **NUR**.
- **The Transport Workers' Federation (TWF)**. In 1910 various dockers' and transport workers' unions were linked together to form the **TWF**. In 1911 the union organised strikes at all major ports, which were successful in achieving better pay and conditions.

Source A: Robert Smillie, the President of the Miners Federation of Great Britain (MFGB), writing in 1915 about the Triple Alliance

The three bodies have much in common. Their membership is considerable, the miners numbering 800,000, the railwaymen 270,000 and the transport workers 250,000. Whenever any of these three great sections have come out on strike, the others have had to stand by and suffer in silence. Should the occasion arise, each section of the Triple Alliance must be ready to render sympathetic action. While the scheme for the moment is not intended to include more than the three trades unions referred to, it may well be found advisable later on to extend the scope of the alliance in the general interests of labour as a whole.

The First World War

At the beginning of the war most trade unionists supported the war effort. Strikers went back to work and the Trades Union Congress (TUC) declared an industrial truce, following the strike action before the war. The mines, shipyards and railways were **nationalised** (brought under state control). Strikes were made illegal. However, the biggest changes were in the 'dilution of labour', which meant the acceptance of women and unskilled workers in jobs usually reserved for skilled workers.

However, there was some industrial militancy in the last few years of the war. This was due to:

- the emergence of local, factory shop floor-based trade union leaders known as shop stewards, who were more militant and extreme in their views.
- The Munitions of War Act, which prevented munitions workers from leaving their jobs without their employers' permission.

In the factories and shipyards of Clydeside, near Glasgow, many union members, whipped up by their shop stewards, were angry with their unions for agreeing with The Munitions of War Act. Strikes, led by shop stewards, took place in several factories. After a series of unofficial strikes in 1916 some rebel shop stewards were put in prison.

Towards the end of the war, discontent spread, and the industrial truce was severely strained. Prices doubled and wages lagged behind. Moreover, the unions emerged stronger due to a spectacular leap in union membership, from four million in 1914 to over eight million in 1920. This was partly because both employers and the government were prepared to give official recognition to an increasing number of unions.

Trade union militancy, 1918–21

Trade union militancy broke out in the years immediately after the end of the First World War. On average more than 100,000 workers were on strike every day in 1919, and there were over 2000 separate stoppages in industry in 1919 and 1920. For example, in 1920 the railwaymen came out on their first national strike. They forced the government to improve wages and limit hours, but not to agree to permanent **nationalisation**. The militancy was due to several factors:
- The immediate cause was inflation. Prices nearly tripled between 1914 and 1920. Naturally the unions pressed for matching pay increases.
- Workers in industries controlled by the government during the war had benefited from a national minimum wage and shorter hours of

work. The miners and railwaymen, especially, wanted permanent nationalisation in order to receive the same benefits.
- Some union leaders and shop stewards were influenced by the success of the communist revolution in Russia in October 1917, which seemed like a victory for the working classes.

The Triple Industrial Alliance was revived in February 1919. Once again, there was the threat of sympathetic strikes.

Tasks

1. How reliable are Sources A and B as evidence of trade union militancy before and during the First World War? Explain your answer using Sources A and B and your own knowledge.

2. Study Source C. What was the purpose of this banner? Use details from the banner and your own knowledge to explain your answer.

3. Produce a mind map summarising the main reasons for trade union militancy in the years 1910–21.

Why were there problems in the coal industry after 1918?

The other main reason for the General Strike of 1926, apart from industrial militancy, was developments in the coal industry in the years after the First World War.

Before the First World War

The coal industry continued to expand in the years before the First World War due to increased demand at home and abroad. The industry was run by mine owners who fixed their own wages. This meant that wages varied from pit to pit, even in the same area, although miners could be doing exactly the same job. In 1912 the MFGB organised a strike for a national minimum wage (see page 98). The government persuaded the owners to agree to district minimum wages. However, this meant that a miner in South Wales could still be earning less than a miner in Durham.

Source A: Two miners working at the coalface in South Wales in the early 1900s

During the First World War

During the war the government nationalised the coal mines (see page 98). This benefited the miners because they were given a national minimum wage and their hours were reduced from eight to seven and a half each day. The coal industry continued to grow, due to the needs of wartime industry.

After the First World War

The coal industry declined, due to a fall in demand for British coal. In 1913 annual coal production had reached nearly 290 million tons. This had fallen to 270 million tons by 1924. This fall in demand was due to developments at home and abroad.

- At home, coal had to compete with other forms of power – gas, electricity and oil. Abroad, British coal was unable to compete with cheaper coal mined in the USA, Poland and Germany. British coal was more difficult to mine and lacked the investment enjoyed by its foreign competitors. Britain's 2500 mines were run by 1400 small and inefficient businesses. They did not have the cash to make the big improvements needed to modernise the mines, especially to buy coal-cutting machines.
- After the First World War, Germany, having been defeated, was forced to pay compensation to the victors. Some of this was in coal, which further reduced the price of coal and the demand for British coal.

Task

Study Source A. Using evidence from this photograph, write a letter to the owner of this coal mine suggesting:
- *how it could be modernised*
- *why these miners deserve reasonable working conditions, especially pay and hours of work.*

What were the causes, events and results of Black Friday and Red Friday?

The increased trade union militancy and the problems of the coal industry brought about two events which almost led to a general strike, Black and Red Friday.

The causes of Black Friday, 15 April 1921

The government was due to return the coal industry to private ownership in 1921 but the MFGB was determined to bring about permanent nationalisation of the coal mines. In 1919, faced with the threat of a coal strike, the government played for time by setting up a Royal Commission to enquire into the coal industry under the chairmanship of Sir John Sankey. The Prime Minister, Lloyd George, promised to carry out the recommendations of the Commission.

The Sankey Commission reported in 1920 and declared itself in favour of permanent nationalisation, a shorter working day and increased wages. Although wages were put up and the working day reduced to seven hours, the government refused to accept permanent nationalisation. Lloyd George broke his promise because he was leader of a **coalition government** dominated by Conservatives who opposed nationalisation.

In the winter of 1920–21 the coal industry was hit by a really bad slump. The export price of coal fell from £5.75 per ton in the summer of 1920 to £1.20 in the spring of 1921. The government found itself spending £5 million a month to balance the coal budget. Therefore it decided to give up control of the coal industry on 31 March 1921, five months earlier than expected.

The coal-mine owners, soon to be back in control, published their new conditions, which included a return to district wages, a seven and a half hour working day and severe wage cuts (as much as 50 per cent in some parts of South Wales). To be fair, the owners were faced with a declining coal industry that was making massive losses. However, the extra half hour a day did not make sense. This would lead to even more production of coal, which could not be sold abroad and would bring down prices even more.

The events

The President of the MFGB, Herbert Smith, refused to agree to these conditions and, on 31 March 1921, the coal owners **locked out** over one million miners. Smith appealed to the other two members of the Triple Alliance to take strike action to assist the miners. The NUR and TWF agreed to come out in sympathy with the miners on Friday 15 April 1921.

On that day, however, Lloyd George offered to re-open negotiations with the MFGB, but they refused because the owners would still not accept their demand for a National Wages Board to guarantee a national minimum wage. The other two unions believed that the leaders of the MFGB were being too stubborn and withdrew their support. The miners were left to fight on alone. This is why the miners nicknamed it 'Black Friday'.

Source A: From a letter written by a miner and published in a national newspaper in April 1921

Make no mistake. It will be your turn next. The miners are locked out in the great war on wages. Are you going to refuse to support them? Your place is in the firing-line. Your safety, your standards, your wages, depend upon action now.

Task

1. *Study Source A. What can you learn from Source A about Black Friday?*

Arthur Cook, Secretary of the MFGB, in 1926

Effects

The defeat on Black Friday had several effects:
- The Triple Alliance was now known as the 'Cripple Alliance' and collapsed.
- The miners were eventually starved back to work in July 1921 and had to accept pay cuts and an extra half an hour a day.

Task

2. *Working in pairs, put together headlines from Black Friday from a newspaper sympathetic to the owners or the government.*

- The long stoppage brought great hardship to the miners' families. They had to exist on 'strike pay' from the union, which was far less than their usual income. Many families only kept going with the help of **soup kitchens**, which were set up in the mining areas to help the needy.
- Some lost confidence in the trade union movement and membership fell by two million over the next eighteen months. The General Council of the TUC was set up to represent trade unions in future negotiations.

The problems of the coal industry remained. There was no long-term solution.

The causes of Red Friday, 31 July 1925

The coal industry revived temporarily in 1923 because of events in the Ruhr, the coal-producing area of Germany. This area had been occupied by French and Belgian troops in January 1923 when the Germans failed to make **reparations** payments. The coal workers in the area went on strike and refused to co-operate with the troops. German coal exports stopped, which meant more business for British mines.

However, by 1925 coal prices had again slumped. The owners, facing great losses, proposed immediate wage reductions and another half an hour on the day. All this was to take effect on Friday 31 July 1925. A J Cook, the Secretary of the MFGB, would not even consider the smallest reduction in wages. Cook had previously worked underground in South Wales for 21 years and was famous for his fiery speeches. He believed that a miner's life was hard enough already and wanted to revive the Triple Alliance in order to strengthen the trade union movement.

The events

The General Council of the TUC backed the miners, and all movement of coal by land and water was to be stopped from Friday 31 July. The Prime Minister, Stanley Baldwin, was not ready for a general strike. He therefore stepped in and agreed to:
- offer a **subsidy** of £24 million to the coal owners for the next nine months to prevent wage cuts. The subsidy would end on 1 May 1926.
- set up a commission, led by the Liberal Herbert Samuel, to study the problems of the coal industry and come up with a long-term solution.

The results

The trade union newspaper the *Daily Herald* put out a poster saying 'Red Friday', believing it was a victory for the unions and a defeat for the government. It was, however, just a breathing space. The problems of the coal industry had only been shelved for nine months. Everyone knew there would be a showdown if the miners and pit owners did not agree about what was to happen when the government subsidy ended on 1 May 1926. Meanwhile:

• Baldwin set up the Organisation for the Maintenance of Supplies in September 1925, to recruit volunteers prepared to take over the work of strikers (see page 110). He had no intention of backing down again.

• The General Council of the TUC made little or no preparations. They were confident that the government would back down again.

Stanley Baldwin, reading in his library

Source C: **A cartoon from a British newspaper, published in August 1925. The large figure is John Bull, the typical British person. The small figure is Baldwin.**

Tasks

3. *What is the message of Source C?*

4. *Who were the winners and losers on Black and Red Friday? Make a copy of the following grid, giving a brief explanation for each choice. One example has been done for you.*

	Miners	Owners	Trade Unions	Government
Black Friday			Losers. Triple Alliance backed down and collapsed.	
Red Friday				

Why was the Samuel Commission important?

The Samuel Commission reported in March 1926 and recommended a thorough reorganisation and modernisation of the coal industry and an end to the government subsidy, which would mean a temporary miners' pay cut while the industry was being reorganised. It rejected a longer working day for the miners, as demand for coal had fallen.

The government, owners and miners reacted in different ways to the report.

- Baldwin accepted the recommendations of the report and announced that the subsidy would end on 30 April 1926.
- The owners did not agree to reorganise the industry. To be fair, it was difficult for them to spend money on reorganisation at a time when they were losing money each month and would soon lose the government subsidy. However, they set wage cuts lower than Samuel proposed and announced an extra half hour on the day.
- The MFGB welcomed the idea of modernisation but rejected the idea of a temporary wage cut. Arthur Cook coined the slogan: 'Not a penny off the pay! Not a minute on the day!' They called on the other unions to support them by coming out on strike.
- The TUC agreed to support the miners and to negotiate with the government on their behalf.

Task

Who was to blame for the General Strike?

a) Make a copy of the following grid. On your grid:
- *Give each group a rating of 1–10, with 10 being totally to blame and 1 having little or no blame.*
- *Give a brief explanation for each decision.*

Group	Rating 1–10	Explanation
Government		
TUC		
Miners		
Coal owners		

b) Overall, who do you think was most and least to blame? Explain your answer.

Events leading to the General Strike

13 April	30 April	1 May	2 May	3 May
The owners announced a return to district wage settlements, a wage cut ranging from 12 shillings (60p) to 15 shillings (75p) per week and one hour extra per day.	After negotiations with the government and TUC, the owners made their final offer. A 13 per cent average wage cut and an extension of the working day by one hour. The miners refused and were locked out by the owners.	The TUC voted on a general strike in support of the miners, with 3,653,529 in favour and 49,911 against.	Talks between Baldwin and the TUC were called off by Baldwin when he heard that the printers at the offices of the *Daily Mail* had refused to print an article 'For King and Country', which criticised the miners. Baldwin was furious, believing that strike action had begun despite the negotiations with the TUC leaders.	Midnight – the General Strike began.

Examination practice

This section provides guidance on how to answer Question 5 on Paper 3, which is worth sixteen marks.

How to answer

In this question you are given a statement, an **interpretation** of some aspect of the history in this Unit. You have to use the three listed sources, and what you know about the topic, to judge how far you agree with the statement.

This is the highest-scoring question on the paper, so you will need to give it plenty of attention and plan your response. The examiner would expect you to write up to two sides in the answer booklet.

Question 5 – analysing an interpretation

Study Sources A, B and C and use your own knowledge. Spelling, punctuation and grammar will be assessed in this question.

'Source A suggests that the reason the General Strike took place in 1926 was the result of the Samuel Commission Report.'

How far do you agree with this interpretation? Use your own knowledge, Sources A, B and C and any other sources you find helpful to explain your answer.

Look hard at the wording of the question. There are two important points to think about before you even start reading the sources:
- Notice the words **How far** in the question. The statement has been very carefully worded. From what you know of the causes of the General Strike you will probably only agree with it up to a point, and partly disagree. You will also find sources that agree with it, and some that don't. Best answers lay out these different sides of the argument and reach a judgement at the end.
- Notice that the question points you towards Sources A, B and C. You must deal with those sources, and you don't have to write about every one of the others.

Source A: From a modern world history textbook, published in 1999

The causes of the General Strike can be traced back to the First World War, the increased militancy of the trade union movement and the problems of the coal industry. However, the immediate cause was the findings of the Samuel Commission and the decision of the coal owners to cut the miners' wages.

Source B: A cartoon published in the *Star*, 14 March 1925

THE SAME GESTURE — BUT A THICKER OLIVE BRANCH

Source C: From an article in the *Daily Herald*, 16 April 1921. The *Daily Herald* was paid for by the trade unions.

Yesterday was the heaviest defeat that has befallen the Labour Movement within memory of man. It is no use trying to minimise it. It is no use trying to pretend it is other than it is. We on this paper have said throughout that if the organized workers would stand together they would win. They have not stood together, and they have been beaten.

Source D: A photograph of strikers' children queuing for bread during the 1921 coal strike

Source E: From a statement issued by the government, 31 July 1925

The miners' representatives explained that it was their desire to co-operate, with a view to a full investigation into the methods of improving the productive efficiency of the industry.

Source F: From a speech by Herbert Smith, August 1925

We have no need to glorify about a victory. It is only a ceasefire, a breathing space, and it will depend on how we stand between now and 1 May next year, as to what will be the eventual results.

Planning your answer

Use Tables 1 and 2 to plan your answer.

- You must deal with Sources A, B and C because they are listed in the question. You can bring in the other sources if they help you in the points you want to make in your anwer. On Table 1, note whether each source agrees or disagrees with the interpretation. Some examples have been completed: fill in the blank boxes yourself.

(Remember: you don't have to use all the sources: one or two might not be relevant.)
- Then judge whether the evidence from the source is 'strong' or 'weak'. Some examples have been completed: fill in the blank boxes yourself.
- Use Table 2 to note information from your own knowledge which agrees or disagrees with the interpretation.

Table 1: source

	Agrees with interpretation	Disagrees with interpretation	Strong/weak
Source A			Strong. This secondary source draws together all the reasons, both long and short term.
Source B			Weak. The cartoonist, Low, is obviously hostile to industrial bosses, including the mine-owners.
Source C			
Source D			
Source E		Suggests it was due to Black Friday, which was a defeat for the trade union movement.	
Source F			

Table 2: own knowledge

Agrees with interpretation	Disagrees with interpretation
Following the report of the Samuel Commission, which led to an immediate wage cut, the miners union was determined to reverse the defeat they suffered in the failed strike of 1921.	Here are some reminders of other reasons for the General Strike. What would you write about each? Red Friday; attitude of mine-owners; falling coal prices.

Writing your answer

The diagram below gives you the steps you should take to write a good answer analysing an interpretation. Use the steps and examples, along with your completed planning grid from page 106, to complete the answer to the question on page 105.

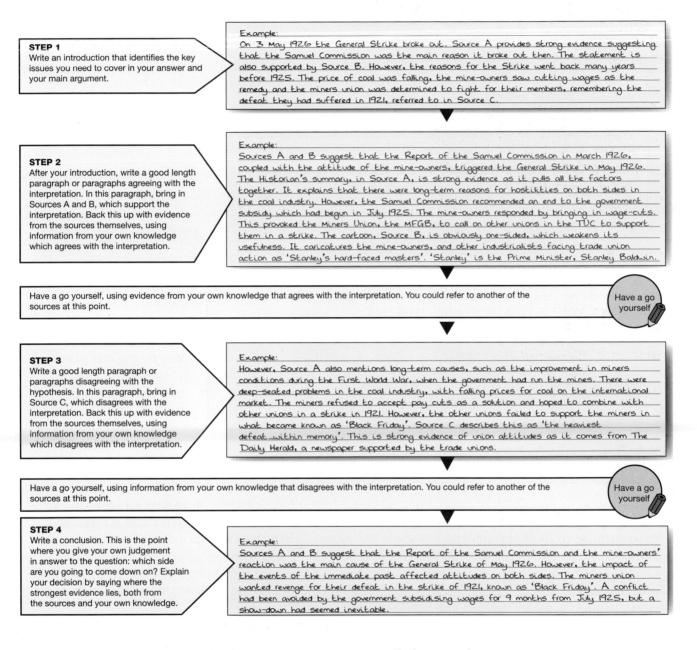

STEP 1
Write an introduction that identifies the key issues you need to cover in your answer and your main argument.

Example:
On 3 May 1926 the General Strike broke out. Source A provides strong evidence suggesting that the Samuel Commission was the main reason it broke out then. The statement is also supported by Source B. However, the reasons for the Strike went back many years before 1925. The price of coal was falling, the mine-owners saw cutting wages as the remedy and the miners union was determined to fight for their members, remembering the defeat they had suffered in 1921, referred to in Source C.

STEP 2
After your introduction, write a good length paragraph or paragraphs agreeing with the interpretation. In this paragraph, bring in Sources A and B, which support the interpretation. Back this up with evidence from the sources themselves, using information from your own knowledge which agrees with the interpretation.

Example:
Sources A and B suggest that the Report of the Samuel Commission in March 1926, coupled with the attitude of the mine-owners, triggered the General Strike in May 1926. The Historian's summary, in Source A, is strong evidence as it pulls all the factors together. It explains that there were long-term reasons for hostilities on both sides in the coal industry. However, the Samuel Commission recommended an end to the government subsidy which had begun in July 1925. The mine-owners responded by bringing in wage-cuts. This provoked the Miners Union, the MFGB, to call on other unions in the TUC to support them in a strike. The cartoon, Source B, is obviously one-sided, which weakens its usefulness. It caricatures the mine-owners, and other industrialists facing trade union action as 'Stanley's hard-faced masters'. 'Stanley' is the Prime Minister, Stanley Baldwin.

Have a go yourself, using evidence from your own knowledge that agrees with the interpretation. You could refer to another of the sources at this point.

Have a go yourself

STEP 3
Write a good length paragraph or paragraphs disagreeing with the hypothesis. In this paragraph, bring in Source C, which disagrees with the interpretation. Back this up with evidence from the sources themselves, using information from your own knowledge which disagrees with the interpretation.

Example:
However, Source A also mentions long-term causes, such as the improvement in miners conditions during the First World War, when the government had run the mines. There were deep-seated problems in the coal industry, with falling prices for coal on the international market. The miners refused to accept pay cuts as a solution and hoped to combine with other unions in a strike in 1921. However, the other unions failed to support the miners in what became known as 'Black Friday'. Source C describes this as 'the heaviest defeat...within memory'. This is strong evidence of union attitudes as it comes from The Daily Herald, a newspaper supported by the trade unions.

Have a go yourself, using information from your own knowledge that disagrees with the interpretation. You could refer to another of the sources at this point.

Have a go yourself

STEP 4
Write a conclusion. This is the point where you give your own judgement in answer to the question: which side are you going to come down on? Explain your decision by saying where the strongest evidence lies, both from the sources and your own knowledge.

Example:
Sources A and B suggest that the Report of the Samuel Commission and the mine-owners' reaction was the main cause of the General Strike of May 1926. However, the impact of the events of the immediate past affected attitudes on both sides. The miners union wanted revenge for their defeat in the strike of 1921, known as 'Black Friday'. A conflict had been avoided by the government subsidising wages for 9 months from July 1925, but a show-down had seemed inevitable.

When they mark your answer to this question, examiners will also award up to 3 marks for the quality of your **spelling**, **punctuation** and **grammar**. To get full marks you need to be accurate in all three of these. The best way to prepare for this is to start taking care over your spelling, punctuation and grammar in the months before your exam, raising your own standards. (These extra marks for spelling, punctuation and grammar apply in many subjects, so it's worth getting better at them.) It also helps you to get all the extra marks if you use special historical words and phrases. In this question, some examples would be: Red Friday, General Strike, trade union, Triple Alliance.

12 The General Strike of 1926

Source A: A photograph taken on 10 May 1926, during the General Strike. It shows police and strikers in Plymouth who played a football match against each other. The strikers won 2–1.

Task

Working in pairs, devise suitable captions for the photograph in Source A that could have been used by the two sides in the General Strike – the government and the TUC.

The General Strike, which began at midnight on 3 May 1926, lasted for nine days and was known as the 'Nine Day Wonder'. There was great enthusiasm and support for the strike and it came as a great surprise to most strikers, and especially the miners, when the TUC called it off on 12 May. This was partly due to the success of the government preparations and organisation for the strike. On the other hand, the TUC was not well organised and became increasingly concerned about the possibility of violence. The miners were left to fight on alone but were eventually starved back to work, having to accept pay cuts and a longer working day.

This chapter answers the following questions:

- What happened during the General Strike?
- How prepared and organised was the government?
- Why did the TUC call off the General Strike?
- Why did the General Strike fail?
- What were the effects of the General Strike?

What happened during the General Strike?

On 4 May people in many British cities woke up to silence. Trains and buses were not running. The leaders of the TUC had organised a general strike in sympathy with the coal miners who were facing wage cuts and a longer working day.

The 'Great Trek'

In London, crowds of people of all ages started to walk through the suburbs into the city centre. The BBC referred to this as the 'Great Trek'. London also experienced its first real traffic jams as cars, jammed with hitch-hikers, tried to reach the city centre. In other towns and cities, there was a strange silence due to the almost complete absence of public services. The first day of the strike was given the nickname of the 'Great Silence'.

The response

It is very difficult to estimate the numbers on strike. Some put the figure as low as 2,300,000, while others suggest that nearly 4,000,000 were involved. Nevertheless, the TUC was delighted with the response to its call for a general strike. At first only the printing and transport workers were called out, with the most likely estimate that 3,000,000 were backing the miners. This was about one in every five or six adults in the country.

In some industries the response was overwhelming. For example, in the London, Midland and Scottish Railway, out of a workforce of about 60,000, only about 1,300 went to work. The rest decided to support the miners.

Violence

The strikers organised **picketing** to try to persuade volunteers not to work during the strike. However, the strikers allowed essential services through and, at first, there was little trouble and only one person was killed in the first week.

Later, as the attitude of the strikers hardened, scenes of violence gradually increased. In Glasgow and Doncaster, strikers were arrested, tried and imprisoned for attacking volunteer workers. There were police baton charges, incidents of stone-throwing and overturned lorries and buses. The police and army had to escort food convoys and buses being driven by volunteer workers. Strikers often threw stones at drivers they accused of being **blacklegs**. Drivers had to be protected with barbed wire, fixed to the bonnet of the bus, as well as a police escort.

On 8 May a bus was pushed down a subway in London. However, three days later, a more serious incident took place near Cramlington in Northumberland. A group of miners pulled up a section of rail, derailing the famous train, *The Flying Scotsman*, which was being driven by volunteer workers. Fortunately the train was moving slowly and there were only minor injuries. The miners concerned were tried and imprisoned.

Source A: A photograph showing the derailed *Flying Scotsman*

Tasks

1. Why was the first day nicknamed the 'Great Silence'?

2. What does Source A tell us about the General Strike?

3. Devise two captions for Source A:
- one used by the government
- one used by the TUC leaders.

How prepared and organised was the government?

The government had been preparing for a possible general strike since Red Friday (see page 103) and realised the importance of propaganda during the strike.

Preparations for the strike

In September 1925, nine months before the General Strike, the government set up the Organisation for the Maintenance of Supplies. This organisation used volunteers to ensure that essential supplies such as food, electricity and gas were maintained. By March 1926, the government had a list of 100,000 volunteers. Weekend courses were held to train ordinary people to drive railway engines and motor vehicles.

People volunteered for various reasons. Many were students who wanted the opportunity to drive a train or a bus for the first time. Others were opposed to the idea of a general strike which could seriously disrupt essential services. Some believed a general strike was an attempt to bully the government and the British public.

Source A: **A photograph of women volunteers working on a train during the General Strike, published in the** *British Gazette*

Source B: **From an account by an Oxford student written after the General Strike**

We set out from Oxford early in the evening in a vintage Bentley, but from Doncaster onwards groups of strikers tried unsuccessfully to interrupt our progress by occasionally throwing stones or attempting to puncture our tyres. On the following day those of us who were to work on the docks received our orders, while others went to drive trams or work the cranes. Some of the old hands who drifted back to work were surprised by the speed with which we unloaded the ships.

Tasks

1. *Study Source A. Why do you think this photograph was published? Use details from the photo and your own knowledge to explain the answer.*

2. *Study Source B. What can you learn from Source B about the work of volunteers during the General Strike?*

Organisation during the strike

By 5 May, the second day of the strike, the Great Western Railway had enrolled 450 volunteers, and by the end of the first week some 3000 trains, about one-tenth of the normal number, were running. Many volunteers drove buses and trams and worked in the docks, loading and unloading ships. However, the use of amateur drivers led to a greater number of crashes and accidents.

The government also recruited special constables to help with the increased police activities caused by the General Strike. The army escorted food convoys and guarded the food depot at Hyde Park.

Government propaganda

With the printers on strike, the government realised the importance of getting their own version of events across to the general public to gain their support. They understood that the attitude of the public could well decide the outcome of the strike. The TUC also produced its own newspaper, known as the *British Worker*.

Winston Churchill, Chancellor of the Exchequer, had some experience of journalism and, using the offices of the *Morning Post*, set up a government newspaper known as the *British Gazette*. The first edition was produced by blackleg printers on 5 May, the second day of the strike. In addition Churchill ensured that the paper was well distributed throughout Britain to get as wide a readership as possible.

Source C: Police protect the government newspaper, the *British Gazette*, during the General Strike

The newspaper was used by the government to portray the strike as a revolutionary movement that threatened the Constitution of Britain (in other words, the way in which Britain was ruled) and the general public. It suggested that the work of volunteers was very successful, that the essential services were being maintained, and that many strikers were returning to work.

The *Daily Mail*, whose article was the immediate reason for the strike (see page 104), was printed in Paris and flown to England, in order to overcome the lack of printers. It supported the government's point of view with headlines such as 'THE PISTOL AT THE NATION'S HEAD'.

However, the Prime Minister, Stanley Baldwin, realised that broadcasts would reach an even wider audience. Regular radio broadcasting had begun in 1920 and the British Broadcasting Corporation (BBC) was set up two years later. By 1926, there were about two million regular listeners to the BBC. Indeed in many country districts the wireless set (radio) was almost the only means of obtaining up-to-date news. The government even placed loudspeakers in many streets to ensure that more people heard the government version.

The Chairman of the BBC, Sir John Reith, decided to allow only broadcasts by the government. The TUC was not allowed to broadcast and put across the view of the miners and strikers.

Baldwin made a number of broadcasts and proved to be a very effective speaker. Indeed, during his first broadcast he could be heard striking a match, lighting and puffing at his pipe to put the public at ease. He came across as the voice of reason who was protecting the public against the threat of the General Strike. At the same time, he made it clear he would not re-open negotiations until the strike was called off. His moderate, commonsense approach won much public support.

Tasks

3. *Study Source C. Why do you think the police had to guard the newspaper?*

4. *Devise two different captions for Source C, one used by the government and one used by the TUC.*

Source D: A copy of the *British Gazette*, issued by the government during the General Strike of 1926

PLEASE PASS ON THIS COPY OR DISPLAY IT

The British Gazette
Published by His Majesty's Stationery Office.

No. 4.   LONDON, SATURDAY, MAY 8, 1926.   ONE PENNY.

ORGANISED ATTEMPT TO
STARVE THE NATION

Orders By Leaders Of The Railway
And Transport Trade Unions.

SUBSTANTIAL IMPROVEMENT IN THE
TRAIN SERVICES.

Government's New Steps To Protect The
People.

SITUATION BECOMING MORE INTENSE.

5. *Study Sources E and F. How useful are these sources as evidence of the General Strike?*

6. *Here is an example of a headline from the* British Gazette:

GROWING DISSATISFACTION AMONG STRIKERS

Working in pairs, devise suitable headlines for the British Gazette *to put across the views of the government.*

Source E: An extract from Baldwin's broadcast of 6 May

Constitutional government is being attacked. The laws of England are people's birthright. These laws are in your keeping. You have made Parliament their guardian. The General Strike is a challenge to Parliament, and is the road to ruin.

Source F: A photograph showing the use of a loudspeaker for one of the government broadcasts during the General Strike

Why did the TUC call off the General Strike?

Although at local level there was a very good response to the strike, the TUC leaders were not prepared and failed to provide the central leadership needed for the strike to be a success.

At noon on 12 May representatives of the TUC met Baldwin and informed him that the strike was being called off. At 1p.m. the news was broadcast by the BBC.

Source A: Newspaper headlines about the end of the strike

GREAT STRIKE TERMINATED

STRIKE OVER

NO MORE VOLUNTEERS NEEDED

THE GENERAL STRIKE CANCELLED

VICTORY FOR COMMON SENSE

The TUC called off the strike for several reasons.

Many members of the TUC were unhappy with the idea of a general strike. They feared that if it went on for too long it would get out of hand and lead to violence and revolution. They were especially concerned by the growth of violence during the second week of the strike. Baldwin made it very clear that he would not reopen negotiations with the TUC and miners' leaders until the strike was called off.

The TUC leaders believed the leaders of the MFGB were too stubborn. On 10 May they asked the miners' leaders to accept the Samuel Commission's recommendations (see page 104). They refused.

Source B: From the autobiography of Walter Citrine, written in 1940. He was the acting General Secretary of the TUC in 1926.

We had all struck for justice for the miners, but it became apparent that Arthur Cook, their leader, had made his mind up to fight to the finish, and wouldn't settle for any terms within reasonable sight. We had brought out in their support hundreds of thousands who had never been on strike in their lives. How long could we hold these men out? When I saw the miners' attitude I felt it best to avoid useless sacrifice. The Strike had to end, even though it could have gone on for another week.

Source C: From the diary of Beatrice Webb, a member of the Labour Party and a supporter of the trade union movement, 4 May 1926

Such methods cannot be tolerated by any government. If it succeeded it would mean that a militant minority were starving the majority into giving way to their will. It would be the end of democracy.

Tasks

1. *Study Source A. Which side does this newspaper support? Give reasons for your answer.*

2. *How reliable are Sources B and C as evidence of the General Strike? Explain your answer using Sources B and C and your own knowledge.*

Why did the General Strike fail?

The strike failed for several reasons.

Leadership of Baldwin
Baldwin played an important role.
- He ensured that the government preparations began after Red Friday.
- He was very firm during the strike, insisting he would not reopen talks until the strike was called off.
- He made effective use of radio broadcasts (see page 112) and spoke in a matter-of-fact, commonsense way, which won over many listeners. He did not attack the miners but insisted that he wanted to help them.

Government organisation
The Conservative government had been expecting a general strike for at least nine months and started preparing after Red Friday (see page 103).

The work of volunteers
Volunteers, recruited by the OMS, kept some essential services running (see page 110) and made it appear that the strike was not working.

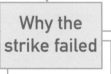

Why the strike failed

TUC weaknesses
The success of Red Friday made the leaders of the TUC too confident and complacent. They made little or no preparations for a general strike in the months after Red Friday. Moreover, they had no experience of organising such a strike. They made several mistakes, including:
- failing to call out essential workers in electricity, water and sewerage
- not ensuring that their own newspaper, the *British Worker*, was well distributed. It did not reach the north-east of England until the 12 May, the last day of the strike.

The attitude of the general public
This was very important. Their support would decide the outcome of the strike. Many were concerned about the threat posed by a general strike and saw the government as being bullied by a small minority.

Propaganda
The government won the propaganda war through the effective use and distribution of the *British Gazette* and daily broadcasts on the BBC (see page 112). On the other hand, the TUC was not able to broadcast, although they did print their own newspaper, the *British Worker*, using the offices of the *Daily Herald*. This was used to show that the strike was working and the country was paralysed, and to refute government accusations that it was a revolutionary movement that would overthrow constitutional government.

Tasks

1. *Working in pairs, think of newspaper headlines from the* British Worker *to reply to those you devised for the* British Gazette *(see page 112).*

2. *Draw your own mind map showing the main reasons for the failure of the General Strike.*
- *Order your reasons, beginning with the most important reason at 12 o'clock and then clockwise to the least important.*
- *Draw lines on your mind map to show links between any of the reasons – for example, the general public and propaganda. On the line, briefly explain these links.*

What were the effects of the General Strike?

The failure of the General Strike had important effects on the trade union movement, the miners and the coal industry.

Immediate effects

Although the strike was officially called off on 12 May, work was not resumed on the following day in any of the major industries. On 14 May the BBC reported that there had not been any normal resumption of work. Indeed, by 15 May, the total number of strikers had risen by 100,000.

This happened because some of the employers in industries other than coal used the end of the strike as an opportunity to cut wages and offer less attractive conditions to their workers. For example, many railwaymen were offered lower-grade jobs after the strike, and some, seen as troublemakers, were not taken back at all. Several employers insisted that their workers resign from their union before they would be taken back. The TUC intervened to try to stop such **victimisation**.

Ernest Bevin, Secretary of the Transport and General Workers' Union, met Baldwin and persuaded him to intervene. In a speech in the House of Commons, Baldwin supported the unions against employer victimisation. This seemed to have the desired effect and within a few days most of the workers who had supported the miners had returned to work.

Trade union movement

The General Strike was a disaster for the trade union movement. TUC membership fell from 5.5 million in 1925 to 3.75 million five years later. On the other hand, there was far less industrial militancy as unions increasingly turned away from strike action and, instead, supported the idea of a Labour government to improve workers' conditions. The number of those involved in stoppages dropped from an average of 500,000 a year to below 100,000. In 1929 the Labour Party, for the first time, won more seats than either the Liberals or Conservatives and formed the Second Labour Government. Their first government of 1924 had been a short-lived minority government.

The government made things worse for the trade union movement by passing the Trades Disputes Act. The act banned sympathetic strikes by one union for another, as well as strikes designed to coerce the government into action. The unions were deeply disappointed by the way so many advances gained during and after the war had slipped away.

The miners

The miners were left to fight on alone and felt betrayed by the TUC, who had not gained any assurances from Baldwin or the owners about the miners. Two days after the official end of the General Strike, the owners' proposals were sent by Baldwin to Herbert Smith, President of the MFGB. Although the government proposed a temporary subsidy of £3 million, they were the same conditions as before the strike, especially wage cuts of up to 10 per cent and an eight-hour day. The MFGB refused to consider the offer and the miners remained locked out.

This caused great hardship for many miners' families. On 19 May the Women's Committee for the Relief of Miners' Wives and Children was formed.

The coal industry

The coal industry declined even more due to the long stoppage.
- Exports fell as foreign customers turned elsewhere for their coal supplies. In 1923, 98 million tons of coal was sold abroad. Exports never again rose above 77 million tons.
- The owners had made even greater losses and were less able to carry out essential modernisation. Coal production had reached 243 million tons in 1925. This fell by half, to 126 million tons in 1926. After standing idle for

seven months, many of the smaller pits were forced to close down.

- Some miners did not get their jobs back because of pit closures or because the owners took the opportunity not to re-employ active union members. In January 1927, 200,000 miners did not have jobs. Within six months this had increased to 250,000.

Source A: Directive from the TUC, 14 May 1926

NO VICTIMISATION!
Resist employers who are trying to beat down wages! The calling off of the Strike was not evidence of weakness. It was evidence of a genuine belief that peace could be obtained on terms honourable and beneficial to the whole movement and the whole nation.
STAND TOGETHER!
Sign no individual agreement. Stick to your unions and they will protect you.

Source B: An appeal from the Women's Committee in the national press, 20 May 1926

May we appeal to your readers for the miners' wives and children who are now in desperate straits? Some of the mining valleys, owing to the bad trade of the last few years, are now practically famine areas. Save the children of our country from the terrible consequences of under-feeding while this great industrial battle is being fought over their heads.

Source C: A report from Leicestershire, July 1926

The condition of most of the miners' homes in Leicestershire is almost beyond description. The children are obviously suffering from malnutrition and a large proportion of them have sores on their faces. They are nearly all pale, while many of them are going about with heavy chest and bronchial colds. I visited one home where there are fourteen members of the family, including the parents, to be fed. Their bread bill is 58p, leaving 4p for all the necessities for fourteen people!

Source D: A photograph of miners going back to work at Newdigate Colliery, October 1926

Tasks

1. Study Source A. What can you learn from Source A about victimisation?

2. How reliable are Sources B and C as evidence of the conditions of the miners' families? Explain your answer using Sources B and C and your own knowledge.

3. Study Source D. Why was this photograph published? Use details from the photograph and your own knowledge to explain your answer.

4. The coal owners received very little sympathy and were accused of being heartless. Imagine you are a coal owner in December 1926. Write a letter to your local newspaper defending your actions during and after the General Strike.

Revision activities

Chapter 1 The activities of the women's societies and the reaction of the authorities

1. What do the following initials stand for?
   • WSPU
   • WFL
   • NUWSS

2. Are the following statements true or false? If the statements are false, correct them so they are true.

	True	False
a. The NUWSS believed in violent methods.		
b. Charlotte Despard was the leader of the WFL.		
c. The 'Cat and Mouse Act' ended force-feeding.		
d. Emily Davison was killed by the King's horse.		
e. Millicent Fawcett was a suffragette.		
f. Members of the NUWSS refused to pay taxes.		

3. Match the words to the definitions.

Words	Definitions
a. Suffragettes	i. Ended force-feeding
b. Suffragists	ii. Women who campaigned violently for the vote
c. Militancy	iii. The right to vote
d. Temporary Discharge Act	iv. The use of extreme, even violent, methods
e. Suffrage	v. Women who campaigned peacefully for the vote

Chapter 2 Child welfare measures and old age pensions

1. Explain, in no more than a sentence, what you know about the following:

   a. The Booth Report
   b. The Rowntree Report
   c. The work of Dr Barnardo
   d. The condition of recruits to the British army for the Boer War
   e. The workhouse.

2. Summarise in ten words or less the following examples of the Liberal social reforms:

School meals	
Medical inspections	
The safety of children	
Pensions for the old	

3. For the following two statements, write a paragraph on each, explaining why you agree or disagree with it.

   Put the statements in bubbles.
   • The introduction of the Old Age Pensions helped all old people.
   • The School Meals Act (1906) was the most important Liberal children's reform.

Chapter 3 Labour Exchanges and the National Insurance Act

1. This account of the introduction of National Insurance is by a student who has not revised thoroughly. Rewrite it, correcting any errors.

   The Liberals introduced Labour Exchanges in 1908 and then National Insurance in 1912. Beveridge introduced the Exchanges and his assistant Winston Churchill was put in charge of them. National Insurance would stop people fearing unemployment and the government took nine pence out of the workers' wages and then put in two pence – this was called nine pence for four pence. The three National Insurance acts would help many people.

2. Statement question:

   Labour Exchanges and National Insurance were of little help to the British workers.

   Write **TWO** paragraphs disagreeing with this statement.

3. What were the following?

   a. The National Insurance stamp
   b. 'Ninepence for fourpence'
   c. The Poor Law
   d. Friendly Societies

Chapter 4 The part played by the British on the Western Front

1. Explain why the following battles were important in 1914:

   a. Mons
   b. Marne
   c. First Battle of Ypres

2. Here is a block diagram of countries representing Germany, Belgium, Russia, France and Britain.

   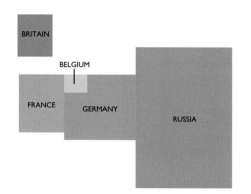

   - Make a copy and use it to show the various stages of the Schlieffen Plan.
   - Use a similar block diagram to show the reasons for the failure of the plan.

3. Which of the following statements best explains the failure of the Schlieffen Plan? Explain your choice.
   - It failed because the original plan was too ambitious.
   - It failed because von Moltke changed the original plan.
   - It failed because of the actions of the BEF.

Chapter 5 Britain's contribution to the Western Front 1915–17

1. Explain the meaning of the following:

   no-man's-land, communication trenches, artillery, barbed wire, sandbags, dug-outs, zig-zag trenches, stalemate.

2. Make a copy of the following grid. Give two advantages and two disadvantages of the weapon/technique.

	Tanks	Gas	Creeping barrage	Aeroplanes
Advantage 1				
Advantage 2				
Disadvantage 1				
Disadvantage 2				

3. Statement question:

   New methods of warfare did not end the stalemate on the Western Front.

   Write a paragraph disagreeing with this statement.

Chapter 6 The end of the war

1. The following account of 1918 has been written by a student who has not revised thoroughly. Rewrite it, correcting any errors.

   In spring 1918 the German commander, von Moltke, took one final gamble to try to win before Russian troops reached the Western Front. In March, the Germans attacked the French and almost broke through. The French line held because the French commander, General Haig, issued his famous 'backs to the ceiling' order. By June the Germans had failed to achieve a breakthrough. In August the Allies counter-attacked. American troops attacked the Germans at the First Battle of Amiens.

2. Categorise the importance of the following reasons for the defeat of Germany in 1918, beginning with the most important in the centre to the least important on the outside:

   a. Arrival of Americans
   b. Failure of Ludendorff offensive
   c. Leadership of Haig
   d. Revolution in Germany

3. Categorise the following statements into causes, events and results of the Ludendorff offensive, 1918:

   - The German troops were exhausted and low in morale.
   - The British were taken by surprise and driven back.
   - Haig issued his famous 'backs to the wall' orders.
   - The entry of the USA meant the Allies would have more troops.
   - The Germans were able to transfer 2,000,000 troops from the Eastern Front.
   - Germany now had a much bigger area to defend.

Causes	Events	Results

Chapter 7 DORA, censorship and propaganda

1. Write a sentence to explain the meaning of each of the following:

   DORA, propaganda, censorship, Ministry of Information, nature of a source, origin of a source.

2. 'Propaganda was more important than censorship in Britain during the war.' Make a copy of the scales below:

   Left scale to show evidence that propaganda was more important.

   Right scale to show that censorship was more important.

   propaganda   censorship

3. Give five reasons why DORA was important. Give the reasons in order of importance.

Chapter 8 Recruitment and rationing

1. Write a sentence to explain the meaning of each of the following:

   recruit, Derby Scheme, Pals Battalions, white feathers, Military Services Act, conchies, alternativists, absolutists, rationing.

2. 'The British government had few problems in securing volunteers for its armed forces during the war.'

   Write two paragraphs disagreeing with this statement and remember to support your case with examples.

3. Make a copy of the following table. Give three reasons why people supported conscientious objectors and three reasons why people opposed them. Place the reasons in order of importance.

	Support	Oppose
1.		
2.		
3.		

Chapter 9 The part played by women

1. Make a copy of the following account of the part played by women during the First World War, adding the missing words.

   Army Naval cooking nurses Air Auxiliary non-fighting land ambulances

   There was also a shortage of workers on the …. as many farm workers had joined the army. Women were asked to sign up for the Women's Land …… Women also went to the War Front, working as ……. and driving ……… In 1917 the government set up the women's armed forces to carry out …………. duties such as office work, driving, cleaning and …….. First came the Women's Army …….. Corps (WAAC), organised like the army with uniforms and officers. This was soon followed by the Women's Royal ….. Force (WRAF) and the Women's Royal …… Service (WRNS).

2. Make a copy of the following table and decide how important each factor was in women achieving the vote in 1918. Give a brief explanation of each decision.

	Decisive	Important	Unimportant
Munitions work			
Land Army			
Women's armed forces			

3. Write a sentence about each of following:

   FANYs
   VADs
   Munitions work
   'Canaries'
   The Representation of the People Act

Chapter 10 The changing role of women

1. Explain, in no more than a sentence, what you know about the following:
   a. The Representation of the People Act (1918)
   b. The Sex Disqualification Act (1919)
   c. The Restoration of Pre-war Practices Act (1919)
   d. The Matrimonial Causes Act (1923)
   e. The Representation of the People Act (1928)

2. Choose one of the following interpretations of women in Britain in the years 1918–28 and write a paragraph justifying the statement.
   • There was considerable change in the position of women in the years 1918–28.
   • There was some change in the position of women in the years 1918–28.
   • There was little change in the position of women in the years 1918–28.

3. Statement question:

   The Representation of the People Act (1928) was the most important act for women in the years 1918–28.

   Write a paragraph disagreeing with this statement.

Chapter 11 Industrial unrest 1918–27

1. Are the following statements true or false? If the statements are false, correct them so they are true.

	True	False
a. Black Friday was a victory for the trade union movement.		
b. The government backed down on Red Friday.		
c. The Samuel Commission recommended a rise in miners' wages.		
d. The government gave a subsidy to the coal industry in 1925.		
e. Arthur Cook was the secretary of the miners' union.		
f. Lloyd George was prime minister during Red Friday.		

2. Categorise the following into long-term, short-term and immediate causes of the General Strike:
   • Red Friday
   • Black Friday
   • Decline of the coal industry
   • The Triple Alliance
   • The Samuel Commission
   • Article in the *Daily Mail*

Long-term	Short-term	Immediate

3. Which of the following statements best sums up who was responsible for the outbreak of the General Strike? Give a brief explanation for your choice.
   • The coal owners were most to blame.
   • The government was most to blame.
   • The miners were not to blame at all.
   • The TUC was not to blame at all.
   • All four were to blame.

Chapter 12 The General Strike of 1926

1. The following are possible headlines during the General Strike. Decide whether they were from the *British Gazette* or *British Worker*.
   • More And More Strikers Returning To Work
   • The Strike Is An Attempt To Bully The British Public
   • More And More Workers Join The Strike
   • Many Trains Running On Time
   • Transport Paralysed
   • Volunteers Doing A Wonderful Job
   • Volunteers Are Blacklegs

British Gazette	*British Worker*

2. Explain, in no more than one sentence, what you know about the following:
   • The OMS
   • The BBC
   • The *British Worker*
   • The TUC decision to end the General Strike

3. Place the following events in chronological order:
   • The miners return to work
   • Churchill sets up the *British Gazette*
   • The General Strike begins
   • The TUC calls off the strike
   • The Trades Disputes Act
   • Victimisation of strikers returning to work.

Glossary

Anti-militarism Opposition to the armed forces

Armistice An agreement for a temporary end to hostilities

Blackleg A person who acts against the interests of a trade union by continuing to work during a strike, or takes over a striker's job

Blockade To prevent supplies from reaching their destination by sea

Bolshevik Revolution When a political party in Russia, led by Lenin, seized power in October/November 1917, with the aim of giving power to the working classes

Bolsheviks Members of the political party in Russia, led by Lenin, who seized power in October/November 1917, with the aim of giving power to the working classes

British Expeditionary Force (BEF) A small, professional army sent to support France and Belgium at the outbreak of the war

Call-up papers Official documents sent to those who have been conscripted into the armed forces

Cavalry Soldiers on horseback

Censorship The checking of letters, films, newspapers, etc. and the removal of any parts that might give useful information to the enemy

Central Powers Germany and Austria and their allies who fought against Britain during the First World War

Chaperone An older woman who accompanies a younger unmarried woman

Coalition government A government made up of two or more political parties

Conscientious objector Someone who refused to fight in the armed forces on religious or moral grounds

Conscription Compulsory military service

Cordite A smokeless explosive

Creeping barrage Method of advancing across no-man's-land which combined an artillery barrage with an infantry attack

Depth charge Explosive device that went off at a pre-determined depth. The resulting explosion could destroy or damage submarines

Derby Scheme Scheme introduced by Lord Derby, the Director-General of Recruitment, to encourage more men to volunteer for the armed forces in 1915

Domestic service Employment as servants in people's homes

Dug-out Roofed underground shelter for troops in the trenches

Flappers Young women of the 1920s who were unconventional in their dress and behaviour

Force-feeding Method used by prison authorities to force food into suffragette prisoners

Friendly Societies Organisations into which people paid regular amounts of money in return for sickness benefits or a pension

Householder The occupier, as owner or tenant for the twelve months preceding 15 July in any year, of any dwelling-house in the country

Humanitarian Having the interests of mankind at heart

Hunger strike Refusal to take food

Industrial nation Country with heavy dependence on industries such as coal, iron, steel and shipbuilding

Infant mortality The number of deaths in the first year of life per 1000 children born

Infantrymen Foot soldiers

Justice of the Peace Magistrate appointed to preserve the peace in a county

Liberal Open-minded; member of the Liberal Party

Lock out When employers refuse to allow workers to work until they accept certain conditions

MFGB Miners Federation of Great Britain and Ireland

Militant Using extreme methods, even violence

Munitions Military weapons and ammunition

Mutiny Refusal to obey orders

Nationalisation Government control of industry

Nationalise To put a service or industry under government control

New Liberals The name given to members of the Liberal Party at the beginning of the twentieth century who believed that the state should use its powers to reduce social inequality

No-man's-land Area between the two opposing lines of trenches

NUR National Union of Railwaymen

NUWSS National Union of Women's Suffrage Societies

Outflank To go round the side of the opposing army

Pacifism The belief that violence of any kind is unjustifiable and that one should not participate in war

Picketing Standing outside a place of work and trying to persuade workers not to enter during a strike

Pilgrimage A journey taken for religious or moral reasons

Pillboxes Fortified gun positions, usually made of concrete

Protected jobs Those jobs at home designated essential to keep the war effort going; the workers involved were exempt from conscription

Poor Law A law providing for the relief and support of the poor by using public (parish) funds

Quakers Members of the Society of Friends, a religious group which opposed violence and war

Reconnaissance balloons Hot-air balloons from which observers could find out about the enemy's position

Reparations Compensation demanded from a defeated nation for damage caused during the war

Salvation Army Worldwide religious organisation set up to revive Christianity and help the poor

Sanatorium An establishment for the treatment of invalids, especially those recovering from tuberculosis

Sinn Fein Extreme Irish Nationalist Party whose members wanted an Irish republic

Soup kitchen Place where soup can be given free of charge to the hungry and poor

Spring Offensive The German offensive that began in March 1918, also known as Operation Michael or the Ludendorff Offensive

Subsidy State financial help to support an industry

Suffrage The right to vote

Suffragette Supporter of votes for women, who was willing to use extreme methods

Suffragist Supporter of votes for women, who believed in peaceful methods

Sympathetic In support of

Syndicalism Belief in workers taking over the government through direct strike action

Trade union Organisation of workers set up to negotiate better conditions

Trades Union Congress (TUC) The official representative body of British trade unions

Triple Entente An agreement formed in 1907 between Russia, France and Britain, also known as the Allies

TWF Transport Workers Federation. Mainly a union of dock workers

U-boats German submarines

Victimisation Causing a person or group to suffer unfairly

WFL Women's Freedom League

Workhouse A place maintained at public expense where able-bodied paupers did unpaid work in return for food and accommodation

WSPU Women's Social and Political Union

Index